TORTURE

PENNSYLVANIA STUDIES IN HUMAN RIGHTS

Bert B. Lockwood, Series Editor

A complete list of books in the series
is available from the publisher.

TORTURE

AN EXPERT'S CONFRONTATION WITH AN EVERYDAY EVIL

MANFRED NOWAK

PENN

UNIVERSITY OF PENNSYLVANIA PRESS

PHILADELPHIA

Originally published as *Die Alltäglichkeit des Unfassbaren*
© 2012 by Kremayr & Scheriau GmbH & Co. KG, Wien

English translation by Roger Kaminker
© 2018 University of Pennsylvania Press

Published by
University of Pennsylvania Press
Philadelphia, Pennsylvania 19104-4112
www.upenn.edu/pennpress

Printed in the United States of America
on acid-free paper
1 3 5 7 9 10 8 6 4 2

A Cataloging-in-Publication record is available from
the Library of Congress

ISBN 978-0-8122-4991-0

CONTENTS

PART I

The Phenomenon of Torture
in the Twenty-First Century

CHAPTER 1

The Incomprehensibility of Torture

We all have a fairly good idea of what torture is. In Europe, many think back to the darkest Middle Ages: beds of nails, thumbscrews, the Catholic Church's Inquisition, witch hunts and burnings, or the Procedure for the Judgement of Capital Crimes (Carolina) of Emperor Charles V. In Latin America, some associate torture with the Spanish conquerors and often with the brutal methods used by military dictatorships against political dissidents in the 1970s. Thoughts about torture often evoke the gruesome images from Abu Ghraib, Guantanamo Bay, and other Bush-era places of detention where torture was used: a pile of naked men, stacked by U.S. soldiers, or broken and humiliated individuals in orange prison uniforms whose senses and perceptions have been intentionally disoriented by scientifically backed mental torture methods.

Although we can describe or define torture, we cannot fully grasp its essence if we have never experienced it. Try as we might to comprehend the suffering of a torture victim, our powers of imagination simply fail us. Forty-two years ago in Vienna, my first-ever interview with a torture victim for the publication *Lateinamerika Anders* resulted in my becoming physically ill. As Erik Zott, who later became a friend, began to describe his experience under the Chilean junta, I suddenly felt the urge to vomit and had to interrupt the interview and leave the room. It was impossible for me, physically and psychically, to enter his world of suffering and torment.

Little did I know at the time that in the course of my life and work I would interview countless torture victims and survivors all over the world. I can listen to and document their testimony and experience, but it is beyond my spiritual and mental abilities to grasp the physical pain and mental suffering of these tormented human beings.

Assault on the Core of Human Dignity

As in the case of slavery, torture represents a direct attack on the essence of human dignity and integrity. Whereas slaves were legally denied their humanity and were consequently demoted to the status of an object that could become the property of others, torture is the de facto dehumanization of humans. Slavery and servitude are the de jure authority of man over man. Torture is the de facto authority. Victims are humiliated and disgraced, often stripped of their clothing, hands and feet bound, frequently suspended off the ground and forced to remain in a defenseless and painful position. They are made to feel helpless and dehumanized, the better to extract confessions or other information from them.

Torture is so repulsive that, following the ghastly methods used by the Nazi henchmen in the Gestapo and SS, it has been resolutely proscribed and condemned the world over as no other human rights abuse has, even in wartime and states of emergency. In order to eradicate it, the international community—no doubt influenced by the abuses inflicted in Chile, Argentina, and other military dictatorships in Latin America—agreed in 1984 to declare that torturers are hardened criminals and enemies of humankind, and thus they should be denied safe haven anywhere in the world. More than 160 states, which are bound by the UN Convention against Torture, accepted the legal obligation to arrest every individual found on their territory who is suspected of torture anywhere in the world. Unless these individuals are extradited to the state where the act was committed or to their country of origin, they must be prosecuted before the courts of the country that arrested them and, if found guilty, punished with lengthy prison sentences.

Human rights defenders like myself had hoped that this method, which relies on the principle of universal criminal jurisdiction, would be a deterrent and that torture, along with slavery and genocide, would disappear by the end of the twentieth century, and that our children would read about this unfathomable practice in history books and not in the daily papers.

Sadly, we were very much off target. Because we are unable to fully grasp what it means to be tortured, we cannot help but banish the idea of it to the remote Middle Ages, or to the equally unimaginable practices of National Socialism, or even to a far corner of our planet. However, my research indicates that torture is still routinely used by the police in the majority of states in the twenty-first century. There is ample evidence that it cannot be relegated only to the tool kit of some sinister rogue state's secret police, because it is standard police procedure in democracies as well.

The Purpose of this Book

This book is based to a great extent on my own experience as United Nations special rapporteur on torture from 2004 to 2010. In this capacity I, along with several different teams, was able to visit a significant number of states and their prisons and police stations. I interviewed perpetrators, witnesses, and victims of torture (in particular those in detention) on the subject of torture and conditions of detention, and then documented my findings and reported them to the United Nations.

It is not my intention to criticize or pillory the governments of these states which, although they were under no obligation to do so, invited me to visit them as UN special rapporteur. On the contrary, I am grateful to these governments for enabling us to carry out our research on the ground objectively and to report on it publicly.

This book does not attempt to point a finger or condemn, but it does try to make the unfathomable more comprehensible and to clarify the causes and dynamics of the routine nature of torture. It could be described as a wake-up call, an attempt to stir up empathy for the "forgotten detainees" and to point to ways of preventing torture and perhaps even eliminate it altogether one day. We already know how torture can be prevented, or at least reduced to a minimum of isolated occurrences. Putting this theoretical knowledge into practice, however, will only work if enough people become outraged at the issue of torture. The resulting moral and political pressure should force responsible authorities to take the necessary measures to put an end to the practice.

The global society of the twenty-first century needs more "rebels" made of the same stuff as the late French diplomat Stephane Hessel who, at the age of 94, called out to us to "react with outrage." Alas, the dream of a new human rights–based world order, born in the Nazi concentration camps and torture chambers and gaining momentum at the end of the Cold War, has now faded amid the War on Terror, among other disturbing developments worldwide. We urgently need a new civil society movement, similar to those that emerged during the military dictatorships in Latin America, or during the Communist regimes in Central and Eastern Europe in the 1970s and 1980s. We need a new global consensus to effectively eradicate torture.

CHAPTER 2

======

The Role of a United Nations Special
Rapporteur on Torture

The "Special Rapporteur on Torture, Cruel, Inhuman or Degrading Treatment or Punishment" is one of the "Special Procedures" of the United Nations Human Rights Council. Just as the Security Council is responsible for issues related to international peace and security, the Human Rights Council's remit is human rights in all countries of the world. Both are political bodies, composed of states and represented by ambassadors or, for high-level meetings, ministers. Since the founding of the United Nations in 1945, the Security Council has been the only UN body that adopts internationally binding resolutions, where necessary including political, economic, or even military enforcement measures. The Human Rights Council was not established until 2006, and prior to that date, human rights issues were discussed and action was taken through the Human Rights Commission, an organ of the Economic and Social Council.

Investigations by Independent Experts

The Human Rights Commission began to become more involved specifically in the global human rights conversation in the 1960s, after having drafted universal norms and conventions in the area of the protection of human rights, including the 1948 Universal Declaration of Human Rights, the Racial Discrimination Convention, and the two 1966 Covenants, which were later supplemented by the Convention on Discrimination against Women, the Convention on the Rights of Persons with Disabilities, and the Convention Against Enforced Disappearance.

To criticize a state for human rights violations or to condemn it through a formal resolution is an extremely thorny political matter, often perceived even today as an unacceptable act of interference in the sovereign internal affairs of that state. At the same time, states are likely to be influenced by political motives when passing judgment on the genuine human rights conditions in other states. As a result, the states represented in the Human Rights Commission decided that investigations of concrete human rights violations would be carried out by independent experts.

When this ruling was put in place, five-member working groups were formed (one expert from each of the five geopolitical areas) to investigate the overall human rights situation in selected states such as South Africa, Israel, or Chile by conducting missions and reporting back to the Commission. Since the 1980s these working groups were gradually replaced by individuals, most of whom became known as "special rapporteurs."

The establishment of these country-specific working groups or special rapporteurs was decided by majority vote in the Commission, thus expressing the latter's concern about grave and systematic human rights violations in individual states. When the findings in their reports confirmed the presumption of systematic human rights violations in a state, the Commission extended the mandate of the independent experts, one year at a time, until human rights conditions in that state had improved. In the case of South Africa, the relevant working group was dissolved only after the end of the Apartheid regime in 1995, and in the case of Chile, it came to an end in 1990 with the country's return to democracy.

Special Procedures

The creation of these country-specific special procedures, which stigmatized the targeted countries, was the most effective weapon in the Human Rights Commission's arsenal. During the 1990s, more than twenty states were thus named and shamed in the course of these public special procedures because of their human rights violations.

This black list included states such as El Salvador, Guatemala, Cuba, Haiti, Rwanda, Burundi, Zaire (DRC), Equatorial Guinea, Sudan, Somalia, Israel, Iraq, Iran, Afghanistan, Cambodia, Myanmar (Burma), and the former Yugoslavia. Even though the Commission's decision to apply special procedures to a state was politically motivated, the black list was in fact a fairly representative sampling of states whose human rights records were among the poorest at the end of the twentieth century.

This "selectivity" exercised by the Commission was increasingly criticized and ultimately led to its replacement by the Human Rights Council in 2006. The Council drastically reduced the black list with the result that today, a mere handful of countries, such as Cambodia, Eritrea, Mali, Somalia, Sudan, North Korea, Myanmar (Burma), Iran, Belarus, Central African Republic, Côte d'Ivoire, Syria, and Palestinian territories occupied since 1967 are subject to special procedures.

Thematic special procedures have recently gained in importance. Their origin stems from the establishment of a five-member working group on enforced disappearances in 1980 because the Commission was unable to agree on a country-specific investigation of this phenomenon in Argentina. Thus, the working group acquired a global mandate. In 1982, a special rapporteur on arbitrary executions was appointed, in 1985 a special rapporteur on torture followed, and in 1986 a special rapporteur on religious intolerance was appointed. Subsequently, thematic special rapporteurs were appointed for specific human rights violations such as trafficking of children and violence against women. They were also appointed in support of economic, social, and cultural human rights including the right to education, health, adequate housing, food and water, such that today the majority of human rights have corresponding special procedures that were taken over by the Council when the Commission was dissolved.

Selection of Special Rapporteurs

Whereas country-specific special rapporteurs investigate the overall human rights situation in a state, thematic special rapporteurs are mandated to investigate circumstances on the ground with respect to a specific right or a specific human rights abuse such as torture, and to do so all over the world. Special rapporteurs submit reports on their investigations, including recommendations, to the Council in Geneva and to the General Assembly in New York. Clearly, covering the entire world is an impossible task. However, through an informed and representative selection of states to which investigative missions are undertaken, it is possible to gain enough information to support a global assessment and determination.

As a rule, thematic special procedures are long-term in nature, but the individual experts who are entrusted by the Human Rights Council with thematic mandates are generally appointed for a period of three years, with only one possible three-year extension. When I was appointed special rapporteur on torture by the then president of the Human Rights Commission in December 2004, three eminent experts had already distinguished themselves in this post since the mandate was established. Following heated discussions in the Human Rights Council, my mandate was finally extended in 2007. Although the selection process takes place through states and as a rule names of potential candidates are put forward by states, the Council, as well as the Commission before, ensure that genuinely independent experts (often from academia) are entrusted with these responsibilities. The independent nature of the position is guaranteed by a number of diplomatic privileges and immunities and by the fact that special rapporteurs are not remunerated for their work. They are, however, reimbursed for their travel and related subsistence costs.

My Duties as Special Rapporteur

The rapporteurs are often referred to as the eyes and ears of the Human Rights Council. In my capacity as special rapporteur on torture, my job during the six years of my mandate was to acquire the most comprehensive set of facts and circumstances possible surrounding the global practice of torture and other forms of ill-treatment, and to clarify the reasons behind this widespread practice and all relevant legal issues. I was also tasked with drawing up recommendations aimed at preventing and combating torture and other forms of ill-treatment.

Working with my teams in Geneva and Vienna, I received and analyzed thousands of individual complaints from victims, their relatives, or nongovernmental organizations, referring them, often in the form of "urgent appeals," to concerned governments with a request to investigate the cases. We carried out eighteen official fact-finding missions in selected states in all geographical regions of the world, three joint missions with other special procedures, two follow-up missions, and numerous visits to other states in order to obtain the most inclusive picture possible of torture, other forms of ill-treatment, and conditions of detention. In addition to producing numerous country reports, I presented a comprehensive general report of our findings as well as detailed recommendations for improvements to the spring session of the Human Rights Commission and subsequently to the Human Rights Council in Geneva, as well as to the General Assembly in New York.

These reports and recommendations, like many others prepared by independent experts, serve as a basis for political consensus-building and policy-forming in the various committees on human rights in the United Nations. The actual influence of the special rapporteur depends therefore not only on the quality of his or her expertise, tact, and diplomacy, but first and foremost on political reality. If it happens to be politically opportune to use robust measures, then reports and recommendations such as these suddenly become very relevant. If the political situation is different, then even the best reports and recommendations will get bogged down and little more than a muted response can be expected.

The UN Office of the High Commissioner for Human Rights (OHCHR) in Geneva—during my mandate, Louise Arbour from Canada and later, Navi Pillay from South Africa—supported my work with a number of outstanding staff members who accompanied me on my missions and other travel. In addition, I was able to assemble an excellent team of experts at the Ludwig Boltzmann Institute of Human Rights (BIM) in Vienna to support my mandate, through funding from individual states, in particular Austria and Switzerland. This team worked closely with the various teams in Geneva and before long became a crucial element of support, without which it would not have been possible for me to carry out my mandate in a vigorous and sustained manner while continuing my work as a researcher and scholar.

From 2011 to 2013, I managed an EU–financed project with this experienced team, aimed, through investigation missions in five selected countries, at supporting governments and civil society to implement my recommendations. In particular, we advised the governments of Uruguay, Paraguay, Togo, and Moldova to establish independent National Preventive Mechanisms (NPMs) in accordance with the Optional Protocol to the UN Convention against Torture (OPCAT), to create professional bodies for the investigation of allegations of torture and the prosecution of perpetrators of torture, and to improve conditions of detention. Between 2012 and 2015, I also served as head of one of six visiting commissions established by the Austrian Ombuds-Institution which has been entrusted by the Austrian Parliament to serve as an Austrian NPM. In addition to making regular visits to prisons, police lockups, and jails, we spent considerable time pursuing preventive visits to psychiatric institutions, homes for the elderly, and institutions for persons with disabilities.

Together with my team at the BIM, we continue to investigate how torture can effectively be prevented, e.g., with research on the functioning of NPMs in Europe, on how their recommendations can be effectively implemented, and on how they can contribute to judicial cooperation. Moreover, in 2016 we began to work on the second edition of our *Commentary on the UN Convention against Torture and Its Optional Protocol*, to be published again by Oxford University Press. On the basis of our research we are consulting and training state and civil society actors around the world, e.g., Germany, Georgia, Kyrgyzstan, Macedonia, Morocco, Pakistan, and Vietnam.

The results of these research and practical activities will also be reflected in the present volume.

CHAPTER 3

===

Independent Investigation of Torture:
Methods

No state is obligated to extend an invitation to a United Nations special rapporteur. If a government should consent to do so, however, it must accept specific terms of reference which amount to a set of basic rules that facilitate an independent and objective investigation on the ground. Among these, naturally, are unimpeded freedom of movement in the country, access to any relevant documents, and interviews with the competent government authorities and civil society representatives. Investigating torture is more difficult than, for example, investigating a breach, of the right to education, health, or the freedom of opinion or association. This is because torture is completely prohibited, always occurs secretly, and is practically always denied. Hence the lack of national statistics on torture. Seldom are there any judgments from criminal, civil, or constitutional courts proving the practice of torture.

At the beginning of a mission, whenever I asked the ministers for internal affairs, justice, national security, or defense; prosecutors; chiefs of police; directors of prisons; or presidents of the supreme court about the extent of torture in their country, in general the reaction was outrage and annoyance. How could torture possibly be occurring, I was routinely admonished, since it was prohibited? When I put the same question to representatives of civil society, I was assured that torture was routinely used by the security forces. Which side was I to believe?

Unannounced Visits to Places of Detention

The solution to this dilemma was to develop special investigation methods in order to establish whether torture had taken place and to credibly document specific cases of torture. To some extent I drew on the work of my predecessors and that of bodies such as the European Committee for the Prevention of Torture, and complemented those approaches with methods of my own.

Since torture occurs almost exclusively in secret, most of the time during our missions was spent in prisons, police stations, military bases, psychiatric institutions, and special detention facilities for children, migrants, and drug addicts. Had visits been announced and tours of the facilities been given by their directors, it is not likely we would have found much evidence of torture. We therefore had to insist on a number of conditions, such as visiting places of detention without prior notification, choosing our own interviewees, conducting confidential interviews with detainees and witnesses, including medical forensic experts on the teams, and documenting evidence of torture and conditions of detention using our own camera and video equipment.

Although the reasons for these special investigation methods were obvious to most people, they contradicted the raison d'être of closed institutions. This led to many governments attempting to negotiate exceptions and, as a result, a number of missions had to be postponed or cancelled outright at the last minute because of a failure to comply with minimum conditions. For example, the U.S. and Russian governments ultimately were not prepared to allow confidential interviews with detainees in Guantanamo Bay or in Chechnya despite their earlier consent.

Even once a mission was under way, attempts were often made to negotiate the terms of reference or to circumvent them. I began to request special authorization letters from relevant ministers in the language of the target country that included the names of all of the members of my team and a detailed description of our rights.

At times, during an unannounced night visit a chief of police blocked our access or a prison director required us to leave our mobile phones and digital or video cameras at the entrance; in a number of such cases a twenty-four-hour telephone hotline call to their superiors resolved the problem. Often, as soon as we proceeded to enter an overcrowded prison cell and requested the prison staff to leave us alone with the detainees, the staff would insist that for our own security at least one official had to be present.

I literally had to spend hours convincing the authorities to let us do our job according to our rules. I would argue, for example, that I had never been attacked by a detainee, whereas the same could not be said of police officers, soldiers, and prison guards. If a UN security officer happened to be on the team, it was easier to convince our "hosts" that we could take care of our own security.

Individual Interviews

As soon as we were alone with the detainees and certain that no one was observing or eavesdropping, we explained the purpose of our visit, our interest in holding individual and confidential interviews with volunteer detainees, but also the risk that the mere fact of agreeing to be interviewed could lead to reprisals. We could ascertain a number of general points concerning detention conditions, meals, daily routines, visiting hours, etc., through group interviews. But concrete experiences of torture and ill-treatment had to be discussed one-on-one, to the extent possible, with the "second pair of eyes" principle playing an important role: Establishing critical trust and maintaining eye contact with a detainee was facilitated if one person asked the questions and another took notes. This approach also made it easier to observe and assess the interviewee. In addition, two sets of eyes are better than one and, finally, the presence of two or three persons (e.g., interpreters) increased our security during the interview.

Forensic Documentation

When we encountered victims with visible signs of torture, and if they were willing to be medically examined, a medical expert (present on most of the missions) conducted a separate individual interview and carefully documented the injuries. I learned a great deal from these forensic experts about various types of torture, the resulting physical and mental pain and injuries, as well as methods of forensic documentation and the establishment of torture methods used.

I realized how difficult it is to feign torture. A person would have to possess advanced medical knowledge to credibly fake symptoms, pain, and suffering experienced in the days or weeks following an alleged incident of torture when examined by a medical expert.

To be sure, a few detainees exaggerated certain complaints or were unable to recall all of their symptoms, but cases where torture had been feigned were extremely rare. Why would anyone do this, anyway—to slander officials and expose themselves to the risk of reprisals? Since I am not a judge and therefore not in a position to determine guilt or secure the release of these individuals, there do not appear to be plausible reasons why they would lie to me. When they did, we were quick to notice it.

On the contrary, medical examinations often concluded that a person had indeed been tortured. In most of the countries we visited, the authorities stated, almost mantra-like, that detainees had made up accounts of torture as self-serving assertions. In the course of my missions I did indeed hear many lies, rarely from detainees but routinely from the police, prison staff, the military, and politicians.

Evidence Brings Pressure to Bear

To counter the lies from officials, we photographed and filmed evidence of torture as well as the filthy and overcrowded detention conditions with the permission of the detainees. When the lies became brazen, we showed officials—police officers or politicians—the photographs and suddenly they became less sure of themselves, just moments after stating unequivocally that they had never heard any complaints of torture. Faced with the evidence, some admitted that when interrogations had not yielded actionable information, they had jogged the memory of detainees just a little by administering a few blows. I was assured by a senior police officer in Nepal, after a lengthy and contentious interview, that "a little bit of torture helps."

CHAPTER 4

States' Methods to Impede Objective Investigations

Cancellation of Visits

The foregoing chapters illustrate that completing an objective investigation and documentation of torture is not an easy undertaking. When governments were genuinely interested in receiving an objective, independent, and, I might add, cost-free assessment of the extent of torture and the conditions of detention in their country, I was able to work unhindered. This was the case above all in Denmark, Greenland, Togo, and Uruguay. Further, Georgia, Greece, Paraguay, and Papua New Guinea showed strong interest in an objective evaluation.

Other governments invited me to come, not because they wanted an objective evaluation of their situation. Their purpose was to be on record as cooperating with independent human rights experts and showing the world they had nothing to hide. They then did their very best to torpedo my fact-finding missions and make my work on the ground as difficult as possible. In some countries it seemed more like a game of cat and mouse with a frequent reversal of roles.

Some governments, such as those of the United States and Russia, tried through persistent negotiations to redefine my terms of reference in the run-up to a mission: no unannounced visits, no confidential interviews, no photography for documentation purposes, among other measures. Had I agreed to these conditions, I would probably not have found any evidence because detainees would not have discussed their experience openly in the presence of both prison staff and the police. In the case of the U.S. detention facility in Guantanamo Bay on the island of Cuba, in spite of the last-minute cancellation of our mission, we were able to complete and publish our joint study on the basis of interviews with former Guantanamo detainees in Europe and other information we obtained. On the other hand, the "postponement" by the Russian government of my carefully planned October 2006 mission to the Russian Federation less than a week before it was due to begin meant that all of our meticulous preparations were for naught.

Fictitious Invitations

Other governments, such as those of Cuba or Zimbabwe, pretended to invite me in order to simulate full cooperation with the Human Rights Council. I learned of the Cuban invitation from the media. In March 2009, the Cuban government announced in the Human Rights Council that it wished to invite me for a visit before the end of that year. Since a mission had been planned to Zimbabwe in October 2009 at the official invitation of the Mugabe government, I set aside all of November 2009 for Cuba following talks with the Cuban ambassadors in Geneva and Vienna. I was in my penultimate year as special rapporteur and decided to give pride of place to these two difficult missions. The Cuban government, however, could not agree on specific dates in November, and at the end of October they informed me that November 2009 would not be suitable after all. We would have to postpone the mission until 2010. After my suggested dates for 2010 were all turned down, I asked the government to suggest a suitable date and they promptly proposed the month of July. I agreed but then found out in June that July was not suitable either because most of my interlocutors would be on vacation at that time. Up until that point I had believed that Cuba's invitation was genuine. I realized then that I had been too naïve and that I had wasted a lot of time and energy.

The circumstances regarding Zimbabwe were even more annoying. In October 2010, my team was in Johannesburg, en route to Harare as per agreed mission dates with the government when the Office of the High Commissioner for Human Rights in Geneva was notified that the "Government of National Unity" was in turmoil again and would have to postpone the mission. I interrupted my trip in Johannesburg and contacted Prime Minister Tsvangirai, who knew nothing about the postponement and informed me that he would gladly meet with me as agreed in Harare. I promptly informed the media about this latest development in a press conference convened at short notice and flew on to Harare with two members of my team, Roland Schmidt and Tiphanie Crittin.

Instead of being greeted by the customary protocol officers from the foreign ministry, we were met at the airport by security forces, detained there overnight, and sent back to Johannesburg early the next morning on the same aircraft. A camera crew from Al Jazeera filmed the unfriendly reception at the airport and immediately broadcast it. As our guards had not confiscated our mobile phones and laptops, I was able to give numerous interviews during the night spent at the airport. Prime Minister Tsvangirai even sent his personal secretary to the airport at midnight to pick us up, but Mugabe's security personnel prevented him from entering the airport premises. This act was not only a violation of my diplomatic immunity but also yet again ensured negative media coverage for the government of Zimbabwe. For us, it meant a considerable amount of time wasted making extensive preparations for the mission, and it cost the United Nations and the Ludwig Boltzmann Institute of Human Rights a good deal of money in travel expenses.

Alleged Security Concerns

Even when agreed dates were honored and my terms of reference were officially recognized, this did not stop attempts to renegotiate conditions after I arrived in a country. For instance, Sri Lanka insisted that I be accompanied at all times by government security personnel because of their serious concerns for my security. I spent the better part of two days convincing the authorities that I would be forced to return home if they insisted on this directive.

Only in the case of China, where I did not wish to abort a mission that I had fought so hard for, did I make certain concessions. In the end I agreed to be accompanied by Foreign Ministry officials during my visits to detention facilities. I insisted, however, that the officials would only be informed of our destination as we left the hotel in the morning. This resulted in a flurry of agitated telephone calls on their part and pressure from our side for the UN driver to navigate as swiftly as possible through the clogged streets of Beijing so that the authorities would have as little time as possible to prepare for our arrival. As a result of this concession, our visits were no longer unannounced and certain detainees were certainly hidden from us. On the other hand, the short notice did not allow sufficient time for prisons to be thoroughly cleaned.

I successfully insisted on confidential interviews at all times, but we had to leave our cameras at the entrance.

Cat and Mouse

The Chinese authorities were experts at the game of cat and mouse. For example, they earnestly tried to convince us that we had to plan a suitably lengthy midday break during each visit in order to guarantee the rights of my team members to sustenance and the rights of the detainees to their noon-time rest. Interviews would be difficult to arrange in the evenings because the staff would no longer be on duty.

In Tibet, the information that the most important political prisoners had been moved just before our visit from the infamous Drapchi prison to the newly built Qushui prison was withheld from us for days. It wasn't until shortly before our departure by plane from Lhasa that we managed to locate this new prison and speak to at least some of the detainees we had hoped to interview in Drapchi but had been unable to find. Our mobile phone conversations were systematically intercepted to such an extent that we were forced to change the pin codes every three hours. The authorities still managed to find out when victims or witnesses wanted to travel from Shanghai to Beijing to talk to us. They were simply hauled off the train and prevented from continuing their journey.

When we arranged an interview in Beijing with Jia Jianying, the spouse of the well-known political prisoner He Depu, she was intercepted at her place of work and taken to a secret location outside the city. When our confidential sources informed us of this, the authorities assured us that she had left of her own free will on a vacation and that they did not know where she was. Once again, I had to threaten to cancel the rest of the mission before she was returned by the authorities and made available to us for a confidential interview, during which we were able to piece together the details of her abduction. It was not the first time this had happened, she explained with a smile. Just last week, while U.S. President George W. Bush was in Beijing on an official visit, she had been taken to the same place, and said she was getting used to this "special" treatment.

Wiretapped Conversations

My interview on 20 November 2005 with the eminent human rights lawyer Gao Zhisheng turned out to be extremely complicated. It all began when he was on his way by car from the airport to our agreed meeting place in a restaurant located in the middle of a popular shopping center in Beijing, when his car was forced against the guard rail by two secret service vehicles and he was threatened by the drivers. Gao Zhisheng was able to continue the drive to our meeting place in spite of the damage to his vehicle. In the restaurant we were followed, and several officials with directional microphones eavesdropped on our conversation. When I photographed one of the officials as he was using the equipment, a ferocious dispute broke out which escalated to the point where we had to leave the restaurant with the officials hot on our heels. This compulsory shadowing extended to my hotel, where it was impossible to enter the elevator or use the lobby toilets unaccompanied. In the end I had to conduct the interview with Gao in my hotel room, the only place free from this unwelcome presence.

I cannot be certain that our conversation was not intercepted, but following this incident I again threatened to break off my mission in order to reduce the official shadowing by the secret service to a level I could live with. Gao was so used to these methods that they did not prevent him from speaking openly with us. Regrettably, he paid bitterly for his remarkable courage (not only as regards these discussions with me). His law office, one of the ten largest in the country, was closed down in November 2005, he was subsequently arrested, held in a secret place for a period of time, and severely tortured, in particular after he managed to send his spouse and daughter abroad in a dramatic but successful escape.

"Clean and Tidy" Prisons

Other governments, such as that in Kazakhstan, were also very good at the cat and mouse game. Surprise visits to prisons by outsiders is a concept that many officials simply cannot grasp. After all, the clutter in one's own living room is tidied up when guests are invited. Surely one couldn't hold it against prison directors if they wanted to clean things up a bit.

Since I always refused to announce which of the countless prisons I intended to visit in this country known as part of the Soviet-era gulag system, the authorities refurbished all of the prisons (at least all those they assumed I might be inclined to visit) with a fresh coat of paint and general clean-up job, and they even decorated them. Prison bands were set up, in a women's detention center a grand party was organized outdoors, complete with music and dancing, and they tried in earnest to convince us that such festive events were a daily occurrence. The women's beds were made up with pristine white sheets, but since the timing of our visit was not known, the women were not allowed to use their beds for four days and nights in order to keep the sheets from being wrinkled.

As soon as the secret service had determined that we were on the road with our UN vehicles, headed from Astana to Karaganda, a police vehicle with a flashing light was dispatched to accompany us, as befitted our status. Imagine their surprise when we turned off at the next exit instead of availing ourselves of their hospitality.

In another prison the disciplinary cells were hurriedly vacated shortly before we arrived and, as we learned during our interviews with the detainees, they were surprised that they did not have to serve their full punishment in those cells. The paint on the cell doors and walls was so fresh that it was not even dry and we had to take care not to soil our clothing with the fresh white paint. Kazakhstan was not the only country where we had this sort of experience.

At a minimum, in many countries, our visits at least benefited detainees by giving them access once again to clean toilets.

Surveillance Methods

There was almost no end to the sometimes bizarre situations we experienced with governments who tried hard to make us believe a false picture of reality or influence our fact-finding work. Without a doubt, detainees were regularly hidden from us, but we were only able to find proof of this in a few cases, such as in Sri Lanka or Equatorial Guinea. In larger countries such as China, Indonesia, Kazakhstan, Papua New Guinea, or Nigeria we traveled by plane, which meant that the authorities could easily find out where we were at all times.

On the island of Sulawesi in Indonesia, we even met a young member of the military intelligence at the airport, whose mission it was to establish with certainty that all members of the team had in fact left the island when we were finished. He was very worried because he did not know exactly what the team members looked like. I reassured him by introducing him to our entire group. He must have been relieved when he was able to report to his superiors that the flight had departed with all of the members of the team on board.

Considering these surveillance methods, it came as no surprise, for example, that the commander of a military prison in Makassar, Indonesia, was standing in front of the detention facility ready to greet us when we arrived. Our reaction was to swiftly split the team into two groups and proceed with the visit in two different places of detention simultaneously, causing a certain amount of confusion for our hosts.

Physical Threats

Some of the authorities' methods to monitor our work or impede our independent fact-finding did involve an element of danger for us. We learned, above all, not to trifle with soldiers. On a large military base in Kara, in the north of Togo, members of my team who were monitoring the entrance to the detention cells were seriously threatened by soldiers while I was negotiating the precise conditions of our visit with the commander of the base.

In an army barracks in Malabo, the capital of Equatorial Guinea, I had great difficulty protecting the local driver of our UN vehicle from being arrested by a furious officer because we had dared to approach the barracks without his permission. In Bata, the largest city of Equatorial Guinea on the African continent, we were threatened by a soldier who pointed his submachine gun at us because we had returned to inspect the police headquarters a second time. He curtly informed the UN security officer who was with us, Antonio Moreira, that he had no instructions to negotiate with us but had orders to shoot if we did not follow his instructions.

In Mongolia, physical force was used against us to prevent us from entering cells where detainees with a death sentence were on death row, awaiting their execution. In Nigeria, the Lagos chief of police had blocked our access to the infamous torture chamber in the headquarters of the criminal investigation department. When we had him overruled by placing a call to the inspector general of the police in Abuja, he flew into a rage and our UN security officer Andrzej Chlebowski had his work cut out protecting us from him.

Counterproductive Concealment Tactics

In my judgment even these situations were not excessively dangerous. They did, however, affect our independent fact-finding options. Ultimately, they were counterproductive for the state concerned because they emphasized the lengths to which states were willing to go in order to conceal their real actions. The more my work was hindered, the more skeptical I became.

This skepticism on my part can lead to a more negative overall evaluation of the situation than is warranted for a given country. I can only urge all governments who invite UN special rapporteurs to carry out a fact-finding mission to refrain from taking steps to disguise the actual circumstances in their countries. In most cases, such measures are relatively obvious and at the same time fuel mistrust, which is not very conducive to an objective fact-finding exercise. Quite the contrary, governments should seize this unique opportunity to have a cost-free and impartial evaluation of the human rights situation in their country carried out by independent and professional United Nations experts. Governments would have to pay considerable sums if such an assessment were carried out by a private consulting firm or rating agency. Any attempt to embellish facts or influence a mission through threats or hindrances has a direct impact on the professionalism, impartiality, and quality of an investigation and should be avoided at all costs and in the interests of all concerned.

CHAPTER 5

═══════

Are Fact-Finding Missions Dangerous?

Journalists have often asked me if fact-finding missions are dangerous during interviews. As a rule I have answered in the negative. It would be a contradiction of the logic that underpins diplomatic relations if governments officially invited independent United Nations experts, who enjoy diplomatic privileges and immunities, and then were to arrest, torture, or cause them to disappear! It should be said, however, that such missions are often tense and sometimes take place in areas where there are armed conflicts, such as Nepal or Sri Lanka, or in areas that are not under government control, such as South Ossetia and Abkhazia in Georgia or Transnistria in Moldova. The United Nations takes appropriate measures in these situations and ensures that UN security officers are present.

In other states, such as Papua New Guinea, Nigeria, or Jamaica, the security situation was so risky because of organized crime or armed gangs that the United Nations sent along security officers as members of the team. In Equatorial Guinea the UN security officers were there mainly to protect us from assaults by the police or the military.

Obviously, even in countries that were relatively safe, prisons are not necessarily the safest places. In Uruguay, for instance, a UN security officer was assigned to me because of the tense atmosphere in the detention facilities. Although governments and prison directors repeatedly tell us that detainees are dangerous and that they are duty-bound to protect us from said detainees, during the years I worked in this capacity, neither I nor any members of my teams have ever had any negative experiences with detainees. When we did receive threats, they invariably came from the military, the police, and secret service staff, but never from detainees.

Risks for Team Members

Members of my team who were nationals of the country we were visiting, in particular drivers and interpreters, faced much higher risks than UN staff members did. I consistently tried to arrange for international medical experts and interpreters for my missions. However, this was not always possible for certain local languages such as Tibetan or Tamil. If interpreters were recruited locally, for their protection the United Nations had to ensure that a service relationship continued with them after the mission. Otherwise, there is a significant risk in repressive systems that after the mission, interpreters will be pressured to reveal information about confidential discussions. In a few cases during a mission, considerable pressure was placed on local interpreters (Indonesia) and local drivers (Sri Lanka).

Risks for Interviewed Detainees

Clearly, those who expose themselves to even greater risks are local human rights activists, victims, witnesses, or detainees who cooperate with us and provide us with information. For any detainee, merely agreeing to be interviewed is risky, even if absolute confidentiality is assured. While we were able to take sufficient measures to ensure that our interviews were neither heard nor observed, we were almost never able to ensure that the interviewees' identities were kept secret from the prison staff.

It is crucial therefore to inform detainees of the risks associated with accepting an invitation to be interviewed. Reluctance on the part of detainees to volunteer for an interview is an important indicator of the level of fear and repression in a particular country.

In China it was particularly difficult to find interviewees in the prisons. I had comprehensive lists of individuals I wanted to interview in China, but aside from the fact that it was not always easy to locate them, only very few agreed to speak with me when I did find them. I remember clearly a female Falun Gong follower whom we located, after a lengthy search, in a reeducation through labor camp. Tears streaming down her face, she told me how glad she was that I had come to visit her but at the same time she could not agree to be interviewed because it would have certainly extended her detention.

In spite of the fact that all governments assured me in writing that there would be no reprisals against anyone who cooperated with us, we were able to collect a good deal of evidence to the contrary. For example, less than an hour after leaving the Terrorist Investigation Department (TID) in Colombo, Sri Lanka, we received a text message reporting that all of the persons who had been interviewed by us had, immediately after our departure, been hauled out of their cells and severely abused. A second visit confirmed this assertion. In general, we have very few options when it comes to protecting detainees from reprisals after we leave a prison.

In places like Jordan, where other independent organizations such as the International Committee of the Red Cross had access to detainees, we would ask them to visit the interviewed detainees shortly after our departure. However, in countries like Equatorial Guinea, where international organizations do not have access to places of detention, this was not an option. It was precisely in this country that I was struck by the desperate courage of numerous detainees who spoke with us. They knew they would be beaten again for speaking with us, but they conveyed to us that they had nothing more to lose and requested that we disclose the substance of their interviews as well as their names in our official UN reports. I can only hope that this courageous move did not seal their fate.

CHAPTER 6

===

Understanding Torture and Ill-Treatment

Torture is the most severe form of ill-treatment and, along with slavery, constitutes a direct attack on the essence of the human personality, its integrity, and its dignity. Torturers have absolute power over their victims and rob them of their inherent human dignity and what it means to be human by intentionally inflicting severe physical or mental pain for a specific purpose.

Dehumanizing the Victim

The aim of torture is to dehumanize the victim and to break his or her will. The principal reason for torturing, as in medieval times, is to extract a confession during interrogation. The police are responsible for investigating crimes, and confessions obtained as a result of torture by the police are regrettably still admissible by the judiciary in numerous states as evidence to convict those who had finally confessed under torture.

A further important aim of torture is the extraction of information, for instance about planned terrorist acts or other actionable intelligence. Torture can also be used to intimidate, frighten, discriminate, or punish the victim. As I have witnessed, the powerlessness and helplessness of a victim are further critical characteristics that distinguish torture from other forms of cruel, inhuman, or degrading treatment or punishment. When someone resists arrest or another legitimate official action, the use of force by the police is permissible provided it is moderate and proportional.

Excessive use of force by the police during an arrest or to disperse a demonstration can be described as inhuman treatment but not as torture. As soon as resistance has been overcome and an individual has been subdued by means of handcuffs and/or ankle cuffs, no further force is permissible. Torture would result as soon as the force used serves one of the aforementioned purposes and inflicts severe pain or suffering.

Torture During an Interrogation

The classic situation in which torture occurs is during an interrogation. The victim's complete helplessness is clearly established through certain rituals that may include physical restraints, a hood placed over the victim's head, forced nakedness, and/or suspension in an often painful and degrading position. Secret detention or interrogation facilities are virtually "ideal" for purposes of torture because victims can readily be made to understand that their tormentors have complete control over them and that they can be killed or made to disappear without any consequences for the captors. The message is clear: "Resistance or escape are impossible so you had better cooperate with us and do what you're told, whether it is a confession you must sign, actionable intelligence you must reveal, or you must 'cooperate' in some other way." Should the victim continue to resist, his or her will is systematically broken through increasingly severe pain or suffering.

Physical and Mental Torture

Physical torture methods have changed little since medieval times and range from physical blows to the most cruel means of inflicting agony and torment ever devised by the human mind. These are described in detail in Chapter 11 below. Methods of psychological torture were virtually perfected by the CIA during the War on Terror. These methods range from disorientation and humiliation of the victims by physical restraint, forced nakedness, a hood placed over the detainees' heads, sleep restriction or deprivation, excessive noise, being kept in darkness, being kept in isolation for long periods and, at an extreme, employing abusive exploitation of individual phobias such as claustrophobia or fear of a particular animal, for example.

Whereas physical torture always leads to serious mental anguish and suffering, psychological torture is not necessarily associated with bodily pain or harm. In many of the torture methods developed by the CIA and other intelligence agencies, which leave no physical traces or marks, such as restraining the victim in unnatural positions, forcing the victim to stand for hours, or "waterboarding," the line between physical and mental torture is blurred.

CHAPTER 7

Inhuman Detention Conditions:
Worse than Torture?

In the course of our fact-finding missions, we visited hundreds of prisons, police stations, and other places of detention, we spoke with countless detainees and asked them if they had been tortured. Many replied similarly: "Of course I was tortured by the police after I was arrested, it's standard procedure, everyone is tortured. It was awful. But even worse are the detention conditions I have had to endure for months or years. Nobody would treat their dog like this. We are treated worse than animals."

Indeed, detention conditions in the majority of states are far more dreadful than most people can imagine. Prison walls serve not only to keep inmates inside but also to keep the public out. Most people have never been inside a prison and probably don't really want to know what it looks like. Their empathy with detainees is limited. "If someone is in jail, it is certainly for a reason" works as a common defense mechanism to block excessive feelings of sympathy or empathy toward those who are behind bars.

People readily suppress the fact that many of these individuals are in detention because they crossed the border "illegally," abused drugs, suffer from a mental illness, were unjustly suspected of having committed a crime, or were wrongfully convicted because the court based its ruling on a confession obtained by torture.

Police Custody

The worst conditions for a detainee occur while in police custody. Every sizeable police station has at least a couple of cells where individuals who have been arrested by the police on suspicion of having committed a crime can be locked up for a short period of time. In democratic rule-of-law states, this period of time is limited to one or two days and is meant to allow for identification, booking and screening, a medical examination, and initial questioning of a suspect. The suspect must then appear before an independent court which decides if he or she is to be remanded in custody (for example, if there is a risk of absconding, suppression of evidence, or re-offending) or, as should be the rule, is to be released.

Suspects should remain free after criminal proceedings are initiated by the public prosecutor and during the trial. If pretrial detention is imposed, suspects must be detained in a special remand facility where they are not in contact with the police or with convicted prisoners. Police custody is limited to only a few days in order to prevent torture. If the police know that a person must be released or turned over to the judicial authorities no later than forty-eight hours after arrest and will be questioned and examined by independent judges and medical doctors, and any accusations of torture will be swiftly investigated by external authorities assisted by medical experts, the risk of torture decreases significantly. The law is actually implemented in certain very advanced democratic rule-of-law states such as the Scandinavian countries, but this is not the case everywhere. Austria for instance complies with the forty-eight-hour legal limit for police custody only in smaller police stations. In the larger police detention centers, suspects are held along with other persons for whom the forty-eight-hour limit does not apply: detainees held as a result of an administrative penalty (for instance, persons who committed a traffic violation and are unable to pay the fine) but more frequently detainees pending deportation, in other words, non-nationals who are being deported because they are in the country "illegally."

Among the detainees pending deportation are many asylum-seekers. They sometimes spend many months in detention in prison conditions that are anything but humane. When one of these deportation detainees, as in the case of the Gambian Bakary Jassey, is so badly beaten that he is seriously injured as a result, even in Austrian police lockups he may be hidden in an isolation cell so that no one can see his black eye and fractured jaw. Up until the late 1980s, when the European Court of Human Rights put an end to the practice, the criminal investigation police could impose a two-week administrative detention for "headstrong behavior" in order to hold a suspect longer than forty-eight hours and in some cases so that they could interrogate him using the "plastic bag" over the head method.

In the overwhelming majority of states, there are systematic breaches of these elementary rule-of-law–based regulations, which had been put in place to prevent torture. Even where there is a legal time limit for police custody, it is either ignored or undermined by countless derogations. Public prosecutors or judges can readily extend the limit by simply calling the police, or the police decide of their own accord that a longer period of custody is essential to "secure evidence," that is, to extract a confession.

Prisons are often so overcrowded that detainees remain in police custody for a longer period than they should. During our missions we heard so many justifications for extended police custody that we could fill an entire book with them.

Detention Conditions in Police Stations

The consequences of extended police custody include not only a greater risk of torture but also inhuman detention conditions. Cells in police stations are designed and equipped for a stay of only a few days. In Austrian police lock-ups detainees sit or lie on a concrete or wooden bunk on which a mattress and blanket are placed when needed. The cell has no other furnishings—no table, chair, or shelf. Better appointed cells, especially in the country, are also equipped with a toilet and a washbasin. If a detainee is held overnight, the officers will provide some food from a supermarket. If custody is no longer than a few hours, conditions such as these are not problematic.

If, however, as in the majority of countries, police lockups become "home" for many days, weeks, months, or even years, the situation is dramatically different. Those who do not have enough money to bribe their way to freedom wind up living for extensive periods of time in hopelessly overcrowded and filthy police cells, lacking adequate ventilation or light and without water or toilets. They sit or sleep on clay or concrete floors infested with all manner of insects attracted by food crumbs. The heat and the stench in these cells are intolerable even for just a few hours. Most detainees spend twenty-four hours a day in these cells with nothing to do and never see any daylight. In some cases, in communal cells, detainees must relieve themselves into a hole sunk into the floor of the cell, and in other cases can only fulfill this most intimate of basic needs at the whim of the prison staff.

In Equatorial Guinea, no toilets were available at all, even outside the cells. Families would bring water in plastic bottles for detainees to drink and the bottles were then used as urinals. Plastic bags in which families delivered food were also used subsequently by detainees as portable toilets and were then tossed outside the cell through the bars. We saw urine-filled plastic bottles and plastic bags containing feces not only in Equatorial Guinea, sadly, but in many countries on all continents. As we approached police lockups, we were hit with the odor from these bottles and bags, and they gradually became associated with police custody, even in places like the Athens airport in Greece, where the police cells were so overcrowded with refugees and migrants that we could hardly find any standing room to carry out our interviews.

Detainees who did not have family living nearby to provide them with water, food, and medicine were forced to depend on charity from other inmates, which naturally leads to relationships of dependence, violence, and sexual abuse. In the notorious Freeport police station in Montego Bay, the most popular tourist resort in Jamaica, we interviewed people who had been languishing for up to five years in dark, overcrowded, insect-infested cells. Even the police described these conditions as cruel, but what were they to do when the prisons were so overcrowded that their capacity for additional detainees had been exhausted?

Pretrial Detention

As explained earlier, detention pending trial should be the exception and detainees who are presumed to be innocent should be held in special remand prisons separate from the police and convicted prisoners. Unfortunately, when prisons are overcrowded, this is but a lofty goal. In most states, detainees on remand are held until trial in police custody or in penitentiaries where they are placed with convicted prisoners. In the minds of prison staff or other detainees, suspects are no different from the rest of the prison population: They have already been branded as guilty by the police and have often already been forced to sign a confession.

In Nigeria and many other countries, we met detainees who did not even know whether or not they had been convicted. Some thought the police had already convicted them. They had never been brought before a judge and had simply been forgotten in police custody because they did not have any money to bribe their way out. Toward the end of our mission to Nigeria, we learned that somewhere between twenty and twenty-five thousand persons had already spent more time in pretrial detention than the maximum sentence applicable for the offense they were suspected of having committed. During our concluding exchanges with President Obasanjo, he undertook to have these people released immediately, and as far as we were able to determine, he was at least partially true to his word.

Penitentiaries

In countries that differentiate in practice between pretrial and convicted prisoners, the conditions in penitentiaries (often known as reeducation facilities or correctional institutions) are often a good deal better than in police or pretrial detention cells. Convicted prisoners often have their own beds and are allowed—within reason—to decorate their cells or sleeping quarters with posters, art, photos, and personal items, are allowed to spend a certain amount of time outside their cells, practice sports, attend training events, watch television, receive visits from relatives, or use their time in other sensible ways. International human rights standards ensure that deprivation of freedom is not only a form of punishment but also, primarily, for people to be rehabilitated and reintegrated into society after they have served their sentence. This policy can only succeed if prisoners are prepared for a life after detention while they are in prison through work, training, contact with the outside world, and a worthwhile occupation during their sentence.

Naturally, in practice, there are enormous differences between pretrial detention and prison, depending on the penal law philosophy of individual states. In retributive justice states, such as the United States, the Caribbean, and Islamic, communist, or former communist states, the proportion of detainees compared with the population is particularly high. The United States (with seven to eight hundred prisoners per one hundred thousand inhabitants as the highest), Russia (with six to seven hundred in second place), and China, taken together, have about the same number of people behind bars as there are prisoners in the rest of the world. These people, many in detention for drug-related crimes, are simply locked away, for the most part, in high-security prisons. Such systems have little time, space, and understanding for a policy of rehabilitation.

Mongolia, Georgia, Moldova, and other former Soviet republics impose additional penalties on detainees depending on their crime. For example, in Mongolia detainees who have been sentenced to more than twenty years in prison are placed in solitary confinement and are only allowed two visits per year by relatives. It comes as no surprise that many of these people become mentally ill and/or commit suicide. Because of these additional penalties, prisoners who were sentenced to death in Mongolia (where capital punishment was only recently abolished) were obliged to spend their last weeks or months incommunicado, in a dark cell, with hands and feet bound, and were permitted a visit by only one person before their execution.

In China, an enormous amount of effort is invested in the reeducation of detainees. Inmates (whether they are convicted, pretrial, or administrative detainees such as the ones in notorious reeducation through labor camps which have only recently been abolished) were subjected to a rigorous regimen that runs the gamut from memorizing the criminal code to doing physical exercises. The aim is to ensure that the detainees understand that they have done something wrong. Some, like political prisoners, who even after conviction still do not admit to having committed a crime, can expect their sentence to be made harsher. On the other hand, those who admit their mistakes and let themselves be converted may enjoy certain favors during their detention, such as the opportunity to practice sports, and can expect an early release.

In practice, this form of reeducation through direct and indirect coercion leads to brainwashing and breaking the will and personality of detainees. I remember well the expressions on the faces of some of the monks and nuns in Drapchi prison in Tibet who had simply given up and had slipped into a deep state of apathy. Only very few monks and nuns, Falun Gong devotees, or determined human rights and democracy activists had the moral and physical strength to withstand this enormous pressure for a long time.

African or Latin American prisons are completely different from those we visited in China. Although they are more overcrowded, filthier, and shabbier than Chinese reeducation institutions, they are filled with vibrant life that at times reminded me of a Latin American or African market. A great number of these facilities use an open prison approach, which means that detainees spend most of the day outside their cells. Inmates who have family living nearby can see them often because they are expected to provide their relatives in prison with food, clothing, medicine, and other necessities. There is of course a downside to this sort of arrangement. Detainees who are poor and have no family nearby must struggle to survive and are dependent on other detainees.

In spite of the poverty, corruption, violence, and exploitation, most of the prisons in Africa and Latin America somehow seemed to be more humane than those in China, Mongolia, or the former Soviet states, where the conditions in psychiatric institutions, for instance, were particularly appalling. I will never forget the look on the faces of the people who were chained to their beds in a psychiatric institution in Moldova, drugged into an apathetic stupor. Or for that matter the three-year-old children with shaved heads, locked up with sixteen-year-old juvenile offenders in a correctional facility for children in Kazakhstan where all of them were regularly beaten up.

CHAPTER 8

Is Corporal Punishment Torture?

My mandate included not only torture but also other forms of "cruel, inhuman, or degrading treatment or punishment." What do most people think constitutes cruel or inhuman punishment? Corporal punishment and/or capital punishment, I would have thought. When I dared to bring up these two themes in my reports to the General Assembly and the Human Rights Council, I came under heavy criticism by many states for having overstepped my mandate and violating the code of conduct of special rapporteurs. Clearly, these two topics are politically very sensitive.

In Islamic states, which use the sharia criminal code, beatings, amputations, and stoning are explicitly permitted. In many states of the British Commonwealth, especially in the Caribbean, corporal punishment remains permissible in schools and prisons. After all, corporal punishment was still officially enforced in British schools until recently. In fact, my teachers in Upper Austrian schools used the ruler for corporal punishment, too.

In 1978, the European Court of Human Rights, in the well-known case of *Tyrer vs. the United Kingdom*, ruled that the corporal punishment ordered by a court on the Isle of Man (still in force at the time for minors) constituted degrading treatment and was contrary to the European Convention on Human Rights. In *Tyrer*, a fifteen-year-old male pupil had been sentenced by a juvenile court to three strokes with a birch switch on his bare posterior for his involvement in a fight on the school grounds. The European Court held that the Convention was a "living instrument" and must be interpreted in the light of present-day conditions in society. That was the beginning of the end of corporal punishment in Europe. In the meantime, at the Court's urging, all forms of corporal punishment were gradually prohibited in schools, and most states have also made violence among family members a crime.

This trend has spread to countries outside Europe and was adopted by the Inter-American Court of Human Rights and the United Nations Human Rights Committee. According to the prevailing case law of all relevant judicial and quasi-judicial bodies working for the international protection of human rights, corporal punishment constitutes cruel, inhuman, and at the very least degrading punishment which is absolutely prohibited under international law. When associated with severe physical or mental suffering or pain, such forms of corporal punishment amount to torture.

"Lawful Sanctions"?

Nevertheless, my assertions on this issue provoked a good deal of criticism, above all from Islamic states. Their justification for punishment such as stoning adulterous women or amputating hands of thieves invoked not only God but also a clause that had been included at the insistence of Islamic states in the definition of torture in Article 1 of the 1984 UN Convention against Torture. According to Article 1, torture does not include pain or suffering arising from lawful sanctions. All forms of corporal punishment under sharia were lawful sanctions and therefore permissible under international law.

Taking this argument seriously would render the entire UN Convention against Torture meaningless. President George W. Bush would not have had to justify the CIA's interrogation methods with dubious legal opinions by the Department of Justice, saying that "waterboarding" did not cause organ failure and therefore did not constitute torture. All he would have had to do was seek legislation in Congress to introduce waterboarding as an approved interrogation method or a sanction for insufficient cooperation. Even the cruelest forms of punishment and torture used by the torturers of this world over the last centuries would have been compliant with international law if they had simply been included in a national law. That would put us on a path right back to the Middle Ages, an era when torture was also "lawful."

In fact, that is precisely what some of the whispering advisers of the Bush government called for, such as Harvard Professor Alan Dershowitz, who seriously proposed that certain forms of torture should be legalized once again and imposed by judicial order so that everything would be as it should and confused CIA agents would once again know right from wrong.

A Conflict of Theories

One way to answer the question of whether corporal punishment is torture is to use this rationale: Following prevailing international case law would mean that any form of corporal punishment is considered to be degrading and therefore prohibited outright. If it involves severe physical and/or mental suffering or pain, then it qualifies as torture. Following the line of reasoning of most Islamic states, corporal punishment is always permitted if it is provided for in a national law such as sharia. Thus, the issue of the permissibility of corporal punishment becomes a favorite topic in the conflict of theories between proponents of a human rights universalism and those of a cultural relativism such as retributive justice. Naturally, the dignity of those who suffer corporal punishment is lost in the shuffle.

Corporal Punishment as a Disciplinary Measure

Corporal punishment is used as a disciplinary measure in many of the prisons I visited. But in only very few countries, such as Paraguay, Jamaica, Equatorial Guinea, Indonesia, and Sri Lanka, did I find prison directors who directly or indirectly admitted as much. The reason is that corporal punishment is not explicitly permitted in their domestic legislation, neither as a disciplinary measure nor as a judicial sanction. Although there is no distinct awareness of injustice as it relates to beatings in prisons or schools, authorities refuse nonetheless to admit to the practice openly because it is not lawful. Corporal punishment has a legal basis in only a few, mostly Islamic, states and consequently is openly practiced and defended. But even a theocracy like Iran reacted positively a number of times to my urgent appeal not to carry out the stoning of women, suspending the enforcement of the sentence. This could be an indication that the leaders in Iran were perhaps not quite so sure that this form of punishment was defensible under international law.

CHAPTER 9

═══════

Is Capital Punishment Torture?

The main difference between corporal and capital punishment is that supporters of the latter, including the United States, China, and Islamic states, vehemently defend their "right" to kill others, whereas very few countries admit openly that they practice corporal punishment. The absurdity of this resides in the fact that the death penalty is, surely, the ultimate form of corporal punishment. If corporal punishment is considered degrading, inhuman, or cruel and therefore incompatible with human dignity, how can the death penalty possibly be compatible with human dignity? Does this logic suggest it would be prohibited to chop off the hand of a thief but not to chop off the head of a murderer?

As absurd as this argumentation may seem to those who believe that capital punishment is as inhumane as corporal punishment, it plays a big part in the legal and ethical debate in the United States and other states with a retributive justice system and that continue to impose capital punishment. The concept of a justice system based on the motto "an eye for an eye, a tooth for a tooth" is much more widespread globally than many Europeans might think. Serial killers and terrorists the likes of Osama Bin Laden, so it goes, deserve nothing less than to die. Moreover, myths abound, such as the argument that capital punishment has a deterrent effect on potential criminals, even though this has been refuted in numerous scientific studies. Cynical contemporaries in the United States also justify the death penalty with the reasoning that it saves on the costs of maintaining detainees in prison.

The Abolition of the Death Penalty in Europe

The ethical difference between corporal and capital punishment is underpinned by legal arguments. When the European Convention on Human Rights was drafted in 1950 as the first internationally binding general human rights instrument, most European countries imposed the death penalty, as was the practice in other parts of the world. An explicit exception therefore had to be inserted in the definition of the human right to life to permit the death penalty. Provided that the death penalty was prescribed by a competent court on the basis of a provision in national criminal law, it did not constitute a violation of the right to life. As to torture, inhuman or degrading treatment, or punishment, because of the horrific experience with National Socialism, no exceptions that would leave the door open to abuse could be tolerated. The prevailing view at the time likely held that lesser forms of corporal punishment, still widespread in Europe, were not considered degrading or inhumane, but it was preferred not to go into details about the degree of corporal punishment that might still be considered lawful. Rather, it was better to let this issue be resolved by case law.

As a result of the ruling of the European Court of Human Rights in the 1978 *Tyrer* case, corporal punishment was declared unlawful as being incompatible with human dignity. This shift led to a gradual reversal of the imposition of capital punishment in Europe. Subsequently, in 1982 (at the initiative of the Austrian Minister of Justice Christian Broda) and in 2002, two additional protocols to the European Convention on Human Rights were concluded, abolishing the death penalty in Europe first during peacetime and later during wartime as well.

After the Cold War ended, the Council of Europe made it a requirement for the former socialist states to abolish the death penalty in order to gain entry into the Council. The European Union also became a staunch advocate of a worldwide abolition of the death penalty in its domestic and foreign policy. With Belarus as the only exception, Europe today is a capital punishment–free zone, as is a large part of Latin America.

The Worldwide Abolition of the Death Penalty

This growing trend to abolish the death penalty was also incorporated into an Additional Protocol to the United Nations Covenant on Civil and Political

Rights in 1989 and a Protocol to the American Convention on Human Rights in 1990. Each year, there is an increase in the number of states that legally ban or at least no longer impose the death penalty. A survey from Amnesty International at the beginning of 2017 revealed that in 2016, 141 countries had legally abolished the death penalty or no longer imposed it, and there were only 55 states that still applied it. At the initiative of the EU, since 2007 the UN General Assembly has repeatedly asked these states to institute a moratorium on executions. In 2016, 23 states carried out executions, most notably China, Iran, Saudi Arabia, Iraq, and Pakistan.

Numerous national courts, such as the Constitutional Court of South Africa, have qualified the death penalty as a cruel, inhuman, or degrading punishment and in this way have contributed to its abolishment. I myself, as an international judge at the then highest court in Bosnia and Herzegovina during the late 1990s, participated in preventing the enforcement of this penalty against persons who had been sentenced to death during the war until 1995, and ultimately in abolishing the death penalty in Bosnia and Herzegovina.

However, when I took up the thorny issue of capital punishment in my capacity as special rapporteur on torture and asked whether, in view of the increasing worldwide trend toward the abolition of the death penalty, this extreme form of corporal punishment was compatible with the universal ban on torture, cruel, inhuman, and degrading punishment, I was roundly criticized by many states and accused of overstepping my mandate. This issue, too, will require time before the cultural relativists and advocates of retributive justice in the United States, China, and a number of Islamic states can be convinced that the death penalty is nothing more than a cruel, inhuman, and degrading punishment that violates the essence of human dignity as the core human rights value.

We need to remember that much has been achieved on this issue by the universal human rights movement since the end of the Second World War and that the proponents of the death penalty, a small minority of states, had already been seriously put on the defensive. I am pleased to note that my successor as UN special rapporteur on torture, the Argentinian human rights lawyer Juan Mendez, has taken an even more outspoken approach by labeling capital punishment as torture.

CHAPTER 10

Is Domestic Violence or Female Genital Mutilation Torture?

Traditionally, torture has been associated only with actions by the police or other state bodies. Even the 1984 United Nations Convention against Torture still specifies expressly that actions can only be qualified as torture if committed by a government authority or with its consent or acquiescence. This language is broad enough to qualify certain forms of violence inflicted by private persons as torture through acquiescence if a state does not provide sufficient measures to prohibit such actions.

Domestic Violence

In many countries today, women and children in particular face various forms of violence which for them are no less traumatic than state-run torture and which satisfy all of the characteristics of torture (intentional infliction of severe physical or mental pain or suffering for a specific purpose, including inducing defenselessness). One of the outcomes of the 1993 World Conference on Human Rights in Vienna was the adoption of a United Nations Declaration on Violence against Women and the appointment of a special rapporteur on violence against women. This led to the enactment of violence protection legislation in many countries in which domestic violence was recognized as a violation of human rights, and also led to the development of new ways of combating this form of torture by private persons. Traditionally, violence in the family was considered taboo and not the state's concern because the explicit protection of private and family life shielded the home from surveillance by neighbors or the police. In many legal systems women were and sometimes still are subordinated to men, marital rape is not a punishable offense, and chastisement of children is a permissible means of education.

In Austria, when the police were suddenly given the authority to remove violent husbands from the home (1996 Violence Protection Act), the Executive found this quite disturbing. It was unthinkable, especially in the countryside, that the village gendarme would show up on the doorstep of an influential farmer and order him to leave the premises because he had beaten his wife. Through training programs, for example those we provided at the time at the Federal Academy of Public Administration, a fundamental rethinking was achieved on the part of the Executive and, ultimately, the public.

Beginning in 2000, I visited a number of police stations, including those in the countryside, as head of a fact-finding commission set up by the Human Rights Advisory Council under the Austrian Federal Ministry of the Interior. We were able to establish that in the meantime, expulsion has become a standard measure by the Executive to provide protection in cases of domestic violence and has in fact caused a serious learning and unlearning process in many violent men.

Female Genital Mutilation: Tradition or Crime?

Parallels can be drawn between domestic violence and a number of other injurious traditional practices that constitute violence against women and children, such as the practice of genital mutilation of girls which is still widespread in Africa. This initiation ritual, without which young women are not permitted to marry, is one of the cruelest forms of repression of women in patriarchal societies. Without a doubt, these girls and young women—who are subjected to severe physical and mental pain from which they will continue to suffer throughout most of their lives—are powerless to resist this treatment because of the enormous pressure they face from families and society. The sole purpose of this practice is their deliberate sexual oppression and discrimination. As long as those combating female genital mutilation (FGM) were feminists and human rights activists from the North, they were confronted with the human rights imperialism argument which countered that the fight against FGM showed a lack of respect for traditional cultures, more often than not shaped by religion.

In the 1990s I was working as a trainer in Uganda on a UN/UNESCO–implemented World University Service project involving human rights for women from civil society and higher level posts in government and parliament in various countries. At the time, FGM was still a very controversial issue. Even women with a keen awareness of human rights vehemently defended the practice. A good deal has changed since then through enhanced awareness and education. In 2003, the African Union itself adopted the Additional Protocol to the African Charter on Human and Peoples' Rights on the Rights of Women in Africa in which all African states are required to prohibit FGM through legislative measures and to take all appropriate and effective actions to prevent it.

During our fact-finding missions to African states such as Nigeria or Togo, when we designated FGM explicitly as torture and included it in our investigations, we were consistently supported by the competent female ministers we dealt with.

Naturally, such deeply rooted traditions cannot be eradicated from one day to the next, and education in schools and remote villages is often much more effective than criminal prosecution. However, states would be guilty of torture through acquiescence if they failed to exercise due diligence and did not take every possible measure to protect women from traditional violence. I expressed this view about torture and women comprehensively in one of my reports to the Human Rights Council, providing numerous examples. Although I braced myself for harsh criticism from many states, above all from Africa, the Arab and Islamic regions, in fact there was practically none. It would appear that we have reached a point where there is general acceptance worldwide that FGM and similar forms of violence against women and children, such as honor killings or widow burnings, qualify as torture and that all states are obliged to take countermeasures. Nevertheless, it will surely take a long time before these cruel traditions are stamped out for good.

CHAPTER 11

Torture in the Twenty-First Century

Physical torture methods have changed very little since medieval times. Only the names of the methods have changed. Strappado, an extremely painful method in which the victim's wrists are tied behind his back and he is suspended by them, is often referred to today as "Palestinian hanging." I spoke with a man who, shortly before my visit, had been subjected to this ghastly form of torture by the Jordanian judicial police in Amman. Weights were even attached to his legs to increase the strain on his shoulder joints. The result is often a dislocation of the shoulder joint accompanied by severe pain which frequently causes the victim to pass out. He was tortured in order to force him to confess to a relatively minor offense and had been reduced to a whimpering picture of misery when we visited him in his cell.

Suspension

Suspension as a form of positional torture comes in many forms. In the notorious torture chamber of the criminal investigation police in Lagos, Nigeria, where we met with more than 120 people, among them three women and several children, all of whom had been brutally tortured, the detainees showed us how they had been tortured with the instruments that had been left lying around the torture chamber. One method was to place victims face down on the ground and to tie their hands and feet behind their backs tightly, putting massive pressure on the spine. While in this extremely painful position, the victims were then hoisted by a bar inserted between their bound hands and feet and suspended, adding insult to injury, in front of all of the other detainees. A similar form of suspension is the "chicken position," not unlike a chicken on a spit, head facing down. In Sri Lanka, detainees reported that they had seen other detainees suspended by their thumbs which had been lashed together with wire.

On this mission I was accompanied, among others, by Derrick Pounder, a Scottish medical expert with extensive experience about the most varied torture methods. He was not inclined to believe this horror story because he thought the thumb joints would not support the weight of a human body and that the victim would immediately lose consciousness as a result of the unbearable pain. However, when we found two Tamils who had been tortured in this extreme fashion by the military, we soon realized that they were telling the truth. Six months after being tortured in this way, they were both unable to hold a sheet of paper between their thumb and index finger. Furthermore, in their recollection of the torture there was a gap in their memory immediately after they were suspended by their thumbs, and for Derrick Pounder this was proof positive that they had passed out. He concluded that their account was in fact credible.

Beatings

The most common form of torture is beating—with fists, iron rods, rubber truncheons, baseball bats, whips, wooden clubs, plastic pipes, or whatever happens to be available. Kicking with boots is a part of the torturer's standard repertoire. Beatings on the soles of the bare feet, known as "falanga" or "falaka," are particularly painful and common. At the headquarters of the Jordanian General Intelligence Directorate in Amman, I found evidence that victims of this form of torture were forced to walk on salt immediately afterward. This increased the pain and at the same time made the wounds heal faster, thus erasing any marks on the feet. However, many victims of falanga, even years after being subjected to this type of torture, are unable to walk without severe pain, and the tissue is often permanently damaged and cannot regenerate.

Back to the Middle Ages

Other forms of torture include inflicting burns with heated metal instruments or cigarettes which are stubbed out on the skin, or electric shocks delivered by a number of different devices. Fingernails and toenails are pulled off, like in the Middle Ages, and in Iraq under Saddam Hussein, even the gouging of eyes was a widespread method of torture. In Nigeria we encountered a group of detainees who had been shot in the legs at close range and left to lie on the ground without medical attention until the entire body was infected. Had our medical expert Duarte Vieira not obtained the immediate amputation of their affected limbs, these men would have died a slow and excruciatingly painful death.

Sexual Violence

Rape and other forms of sexual torture against women as well as men are also widely used because victims are profoundly humiliated through these practices. The United States intentionally used female staff to carry out forced nudity and sexual forms of torture on devout Muslim men. From 1992 to 1995, during the ethnic cleansing in Bosnia and Herzegovina, more than fifty thousand Muslim women were raped by Bosnian Serb militias, policemen, and soldiers. These rapes had a perfidious intent, which was to force the women to give birth to a Bosnian Serb baby ("I am going to knock you up with a Chetnik") as a way of humiliating the entire Muslim community.

These represent typical cases of torture for the purpose of sexual and ethnic-religious discrimination. After the war, many women who survived these mass rapes and gave birth were ostracized from the Muslim community because of their mixed-race children, or were forced to give up the children. The impoverished Bosnian orphanages were full of these children who today, as adults, are wondering what happened to their parents.

Asphyxiation

Other forms of torture were designed to simulate the feeling of suffocation. In Paraguay, during interrogations detainees' heads were covered with a plastic bag and tied so tightly that they almost passed out. At the same time their testicles were severely beaten or squeezed, causing extreme pain, fear, and anxiety. If they managed to bite through the plastic bag, two additional bags were placed on top of the first. Waterboarding as used against suspected terrorists by the CIA, harkens back to the time of the Spanish Inquisition.

Victims were tied to a plank and dunked in water with the head facing down until they feared they were about to drown. In the Latin American version of this "submarino," the victim's head was often immersed into water contaminated with urine, feces, and vomit. Waterboarding as practiced by the United States involved pouring water over a cloth covering the face and nose until the victim experienced the sensation of suffocating or drowning.

There is virtually no end to the list of physical torture methods, all of which cause enormous fear and anxiety as well as severe psychological anguish and suffering. Regrettably, the human imagination seems to be limitless when it comes to inventing ever more cruel types of torture.

Psychological Torture Methods

The same could be said about the nonphysical or psychological torture methods, as perfected above all by the United States during the War on Terror under President George W. Bush. The Bush government, basing itself on extremely dubious "expert opinions" from the Justice Department, stubbornly insisted that these methods did not constitute torture. Numerous interviews with former Guantanamo Bay detainees or former inmates from CIA secret prisons ("black sites") indicated that the carefully planned forms of psychological torture, developed by trained psychologists, often caused much greater pain and suffering than physical torture. This form of torture is aimed at systematically breaking the will of an individual through persistent confusion and uncertainty, disorientation, and distress.

Many of the men from all over the world who were suspected of terrorism (some of whom were ultimately found innocent) were driven to the edge of insanity in Guantanamo Bay because they were systematically deprived of all of their rights and held in a state of complete ambiguity and uncertainty. They had no access to lawyers, were not permitted to correspond with anyone, were often held for months at a time in incommunicado detention, and were intentionally disoriented. When they asked why they had been arrested and how long they were going to be held, they were told that nobody knew why but that they would probably have to remain in custody until the end of the War on Terror.

A good number of detainees were placed for weeks at a time in the "frequent flyer" program, which involved moving them to different cells every hour or even more often. When they tried to fall asleep, they were immediately woken up. There was harsh lighting in the cells at all times and loud American rock or heavy-metal music was played often.

"Exposure to extreme temperatures" was one of the torture methods explicitly prescribed by Defense Secretary Donald Rumsfeld. It ranged from open cells in "Camp X-Ray," with full exposure to the torrid Cuban sun, to several days spent naked and without a blanket or anything to cover themselves, in a container with the air conditioning on full blast. Several former detainees assured me that this method used in Guantanamo was the worst of them all: they froze miserably and could do nothing about it.

Another explicitly prescribed interrogation method was the targeted exploitation of phobias, such as claustrophobia or fear of dogs, as revealed by a prior psychological evaluation.

The CIA-run "prison of darkness" in Kabul was particularly awful. An ex-detainee described to me how he had spent almost eleven months in solitary confinement, chained most of the time, in complete darkness, and incessantly subjected to extremely loud noise. He added with a grin that anyone who survived this prison without going insane was immune to fear. I was curious to know how he had endured this traumatic experience, and he responded that his three crutches had been his sense of humor, autogenic training, and his unshakable religious faith.

CHAPTER 12

Why Torture?

One element in the definition of torture stipulates that severe pain or suffering is inflicted on a defenseless person for a specific purpose. Article 1 of the United Nations Convention against Torture specifies the most important purposes of torture, namely to obtain a confession or other information, but also to intimidate, punish, or discriminate against a victim. Historically, the only reason for the legal permissibility of torture was the extraction of a confession or other relevant information such as witness testimony in a criminal trial. Extracted confessions contributed little to ascertaining the truth, and this fact, together with the influence of rationalism, led to the gradual elimination of torture from all criminal proceedings. Over the course of the eighteenth and nineteenth centuries it was abolished.

Extracting a Confession

Although it is irrational to use torture as a source of evidence, this is precisely what continues to occur in many countries in the world today. More than 90 percent of the torture victims I interviewed over the six years I served as UN special rapporteur were tortured solely because they would not admit to a crime they were suspected of having committed. Guilty or not, their admission stopped the torture. What usually followed was a written confession and a clause stating that the confession had been made of their own free will. If they dared to retract their confession in court or accuse the police of having tortured them, the victims were usually turned back over to the police to "establish the truth" instead of bringing a charge of torture against the incriminated police officers.

I have often wondered how this archaic and completely irrational method of establishing the truth in a trial could be so widespread in the twenty-first century and how, in many states, it is the most important means of producing evidence that leads to convictions. The answer, regrettably, is far more basic than might be expected. In the majority of states today, the criminal justice system simply does not function as it should or, at best, is seriously flawed. The independence of the courts from powerful interests is still problematic and, unfortunately, the judiciary is one of the most corrupt sectors of government.

Crime is on the rise in many states, and calls for a more energetic criminal justice system are increasing commensurately. Politicians, the media, prosecutors, and judges all exert considerable pressure on the police to solve crimes swiftly so that the guilty can be duly sentenced. The police, however, are often badly paid and poorly trained and equipped. They do not have modern methods for establishing the truth such as DNA testing and instead resort to the medieval approach in which confessions represent key evidence. Frequently, the police are paid according to the number of crimes they "solve."

The main responsibility for fighting crime in many countries rests on the shoulders of the police. As soon as the police have "convicted" someone, the crime has been "solved." Prosecutors and courts merely validate the confession obtained during police custody.

Find a "Victim"

Anyone with enough money can easily navigate through such corrupt criminal justice systems. The affluent usually are not even arrested in the first place or can easily and swiftly buy their way out of police custody. If need be, prosecutors, courts, or prison directors can be bribed. The consequence of this is that detention and torture, in many states, becomes a "privilege of the poor."

When a crime is committed, the police often look for a suitable victim from among the poor, such as the homeless, the unemployed, ex-offenders, minorities, or otherwise marginalized individuals, and when they find one he is beaten until he confesses to the crime. This depiction may seem clichéd and oversimplified, and I have long been reluctant to accept this simplistic explanatory pattern for the widespread practice of torture. I have, however, been proven wrong time after time. The level of corruption and the lack of independence of the judiciary in the majority of states today are the most important reasons for the persistence of torture in the twenty-first century.

Obtaining Information Under Duress

Other reasons for the persistence of torture play a much less significant role. The CIA and other intelligence agencies do not torture to extract confessions but rather because they hope to obtain important information through torture in the fight against or prevention of global terror or organized crime. Experienced intelligence agents certainly are aware that torture is not a particularly effective way of establishing the truth. In some cases the fear of torture can lead to a significant clue which is then explored further. The fact that numerous clues simultaneously obtained through torture can have agents following spurious trails is deliberately tolerated. An example of this is the alleged presence of weapons of mass destruction in Iraq under Saddam Hussein.

Showing "Who's in Charge"

Apart from its primary function as a tool for obtaining confessions and information under duress, torture also serves other purposes. The very first blows during arrest or the threat of a particularly painful type of torture are meant primarily to intimidate. Other reasons might be the punishment of alleged offenders, discrimination against particularly hated groups such as foreigners or members of minorities, or even more broadly, the propagation of fear and terror among the general public. The intent is to show detainees who's in charge from the very outset. An initiation ritual, often known as a "welcome party," is a feature of many prisons: Newcomers are placed in solitary confinement or in dark cells for a week and regularly beaten so that they quickly learn the rules of detention, become accustomed to their helplessness, and realize they are not in a "hotel." Showing victims "who's boss," alongside discrimination, is often the reason behind a host of horrible actions: women raped by the police, prison staff, traffickers, or their spouses; domestic violence against women and children; traditional practices such as FGM, widow burnings, or corporal punishment of unruly children.

CHAPTER 13

Is There Ever a Justification for Torture?

During the War on Terror, as it came to be known, the United States in particular triggered a discussion which it was assumed by now would have long since become a thing of the past. If the CIA is holding a person who has the code to a dirty bomb that, if triggered, would cause the death of thousands of innocent people, and this person is not willing to give up the information, then surely torturing this person just a little to save the lives of so many innocent people must be justifiable. The human right of terrorists not to be tortured cannot possibly be more important than the right to life of innocent people. Put in more general terms, the right to the national security of the United States surely must trump the liberty and human dignity of a couple of terrorists.

The Discussion Surrounding "Rescue-Torture"

In Germany, "rescue-torture," as it is known, has been a subject of discussion in both political and to some extent legal circles. In the United States, Harvard Professor Alan Dershowitz achieved dubious fame with his defense of torture. His reasoning rests on the straightforward assumption that any self-respecting American police or intelligence officer, faced with such a moral dilemma, would resort to torture to protect innocent lives. Further, it would be preferable if they did not have to shoulder such a heavy burden without judicial back-up and rule-of-law guarantees. In other words, the difficult decision to torture when, in particular, a greater good such as national security is at stake, should not be left up to a police officer, soldier, or CIA agent, but should be regulated by law and sanctioned by a court such that the correctness of the action is ensured and the rule-of-law state is not undermined. Naturally, specific, less severe torture methods should be legalized in order to keep within bounds the violation of the terrorists' human dignity.

On the surface, this sort of reasoning has a plausible ring to it, and almost every lecture or presentation I have given on the subject of torture has prompted the famous "ticking bomb" question. If you scratch the surface, though, it is clear that this logic takes you right back to the darkest Middle Ages where, for example, in the Criminal Procedure Code of Emperor Charles V, there were a significant amount of procedural provisions to determine which torture method, including intensity and duration, should be inflicted for each crime committed.

What happens if a terrorist still won't disclose the code to the dirty bomb after being tortured for five minutes with electric shocks up to 20 volts? How many shocks can I administer and at what current levels and for how long? Do the intensity and duration depend on how many people I am trying to rescue? What sort of information should I provide to the court to ensure that it has sufficient grounds to authorize torture? Should judges be present when torture is administered? With what level of detail should the practice of torture be regulated in the criminal procedure code in order to preclude arbitrariness? How broad should the margin of discretion of the court or the executive be? If a terrorist still won't cooperate, would a telephone call to the court suffice to increase the intensity and duration of the electric shocks? Should torture be used only to prevent a terrorist act or can it be used to combat organized crime, to prevent an armed bank robbery or a cold-blooded murder? Would I be allowed to torture someone who has kidnapped an innocent child in order to save the life of that child?

The Jacob von Metzler Case

The last question was the focus of sustained debate in the German public and justice system not long ago. Jacob von Metzler, eleven-year-old son of a well-known banker, was kidnapped for ransom in 2002 by Magnus Gaefgen. Gaefgen readily admitted the crime to the Frankfurt police but refused to reveal the whereabouts of the child. He repeatedly sent the police to the wrong location. Fearing that the child could die before he was found, the deputy chief of police, Wolfgang Daschner, decided to use the threat of torture against Gaefgen. This decision was successful to the extent that Gaefgen immediately disclosed the location of the boy who, sadly, was found dead because his kidnapper had murdered him immediately after abducting him. The issue that now had to be resolved was the criminal responsibility of Wolfgang Daschner, who had ordered that the threat of torture be used to try to save the life of the child. The Frankfurt district court made what I consider to be the only fair ruling, namely, that Wolfgang Daschner was found guilty of the crime of threatening the use of torture but received a minimal sentence due to mitigating circumstances.

The Danger of Qualifying the Prohibition to Torture

History teaches us that as soon as torture is authorized for exceptional situations, it quickly becomes the norm. The Bush government would have been better advised not to have opened this Pandora's box and in the extremely rare "ticking bomb" scenario to have accepted the possibility that some individuals might not be saved through "rescue-torture." The relativization of the prohibition to torture by the Bush government and its political, media, and scientific supporters caused an enormous amount of practically irrevocable damage to the hard-won achievements in international law and human rights. Moreover, it seriously undermined the moral authority of the West with respect to human rights issues.

For the extremely rare exceptions in which law enforcement officials like the Frankfurt Deputy Chief of Police Daschner violate the ban on torture for sincere motives, there is no need to qualify the torture prohibition and to justify torture. It would suffice to acknowledge the existence of mitigating circumstances.

CHAPTER 14

George Bush's War on Terror

It is not at all surprising that the United States resorted to torture in its War on Terror which George W. Bush declared as a reaction to the horrific terrorist attack on U.S. soil on September 11, 2001. After all, the United States set up its own torture training center in Panama in connection with its national security doctrine in the 1970s and 1980s. Its purpose was to help install and support brutal military dictatorships to combat leftist guerrilla movements throughout Latin America.

Like several other states, the United States secretly employed torture and always publicly denied the practice. George W. Bush was the first president to openly admit to the use of torture, and through his brazen attempts to justify this crime he caused enormous damage to the international fight against torture. Dictators, members of the military, and intelligence operatives the world over, who had always tortured secretly, suddenly received a seal of approval thanks to Bush, Cheney, Rumsfeld, Gonzales, and other high-level U.S. officials. During my missions, the refrain I heard sadly time and again from high-level governmental authorities all over the world went something like this: "If the greatest superpower in the world, which has championed the cause of human rights since the American revolution over 200 years ago and constantly admonishes other states to respect human rights, can openly torture, then surely it cannot be so bad if we torture too."

To make matters worse, during its War on Terror the Bush government worked closely with certain states in the Arab and Islamic regions that were notorious for their brutal torture methods. While the U.S. State Department in its yearly Human Rights Reports to Congress was castigating torture methods used in Morocco, Egypt, Jordan, Syria, Afghanistan, or Pakistan, the CIA was sending terrorism suspects on secret flights to precisely those countries to be tortured. It was hardly surprising that the president of the Jordanian parliament asked me why I was investigating torture in his country, and not in the United States. He was astonished to hear that not long before, the U.S. government had refused my request to interview Guantanamo Bay detainees confidentially.

Deception by the Bush Government

The ways in which the Bush government circumvented international law in general and the prohibition to torture in particular would have made Machiavelli proud. A comprehensive description of the deception the Bush strategists used to clear the path for their "war" by creating a legal vacuum would be beyond the scope of this book. Suffice it to outline a few of the cornerstones of this strategy.

The expression War on Terror was meant as more than a euphemism. The Bush government wanted to make it clear to the world, in deadly earnest, that since September 2001 it was involved in a global war. The war was not only against the Taliban regime in Afghanistan (which, in exercise of the right to self-defense had been approved by the UN Security Council), but it was being waged against the global Al Qaida terrorist network and other terrorists wherever they may be.

Anyone suspected of terrorism could be held in U.S. prison camps such as Guantanamo Bay as "illegal enemy combatants" indefinitely and without being charged. This war was to last as long as it took to defeat global terrorism once and for all, and as a result, illegal enemy combatants could be held until that had been achieved.

Although international law expressly provides for human rights to be applicable not only in peacetime but also during armed conflicts, the Bush government adopted the absurd legal position that the entire internationally binding human rights protection system simply did not apply to the War on Terror. Instead, the "law of war" was in effect, i.e., international humanitarian law under the Geneva Conventions.

Under the Geneva Conventions, people are either combatants or civilians: A combatant is a soldier who is armed and fights against another soldier and may therefore be killed, whereas a civilian enjoys all of the rights associated with that status, in particular the right not to be killed. But combatants, under international humanitarian law, also have specific rights, and one of these is that they may not be tortured. If they are captured, they have certain rights as prisoners of war, such as the right to food, medical attention, and humane treatment during captivity.

In order to circumvent even these minimal obligations, the Bush government created a third category of people, "illegal enemy combatants" (not recognized under international law), for terrorism suspects.

The next problem was that, on U.S. soil, the venerable United States Constitution, which includes fundamental rights such as the ban on torture and the right to due process, in principle applied to all. The solution was to set up prisoner camps or detention centers outside the United States, such as Guantanamo Bay in Cuba or secret prisons all over the world, for "illegal enemy combatants," and to declare that the U.S. Constitution, at least with respect to non-nationals, had no validity in those places.

International criticism was simply disregarded, and it took some time before the U.S. justice system was able to see through the scam. In the case of *Rasul vs. Bush* in 2004, the U.S. Supreme Court ruled that the Constitution applied to Guantanamo Bay. Since that decision was handed down, Guantanamo detainees for the first time at least had U.S. lawyers as counsel.

Far-Fetched Legal Opinions

The absolute prohibition of torture was recognized as an axiom of binding customary international law, and the United States under the government of George H. W. Bush had ratified the UN Convention against Torture, which expressly specifies that torture cannot be justified under any circumstances. Moreover, the UN definition of torture had been incorporated verbatim in U.S. criminal legislation. The way around these rules involved inventive lawyers working with the U.S. Justice Department, among them John Yoo and Jay Bybee, who wrote fanciful legal opinions aimed at limiting the concept of torture to extremely cruel methods which cause organ failure, death, or irreversible mental damage. This new U.S. definition would not include "normal" torture methods such as waterboarding or similar "enhanced interrogation techniques" of the CIA.

The legal opinion was discreetly withdrawn in 2004 when it became known that systematic torture was being used in the Abu Ghraib U.S. prison in Iraq, but served to buttress the way, for instance, that Defense Secretary Donald Rumsfeld spelled out precisely which interrogation methods were permissible in Guantanamo Bay. These included prolonged standing in stress positions, sleep deprivation lasting several weeks, the exploitation of specific individual phobias such as claustrophobia or the fear of dogs, exposure to extreme temperatures, deliberate disorientation, among others.

In a UN report that I, in collaboration with four other experts, published at the beginning of 2006, we were able to expose in detail the torture methods used and the unlawfulness of the entire Guantanamo Bay detention camp. Our research was based on documents available at the time and numerous interviews conducted with former Guantanamo prisoners, and we were the first international entity to demand that the camp be closed down immediately. Regrettably, the Obama government failed, in spite of its pledges, to shut down this facility which had become a symbol of lawlessness in the War on Terror. It also failed to prosecute those responsible for torture and its justification and to compensate the victims of torture and arbitrary detention.

Secret Detention in Foreign Prisons

When the interrogation methods permissible in the United States did not yield results, the prisoners were sent for interrogation on clandestine CIA flights to friendly countries notorious for their torture methods, such as Egypt, Morocco, or Syria, under the "extraordinary rendition" program. In order to circumvent International Aviation Law, which has specific regulations for official state airlines, the CIA used private air carriers to charter aircraft for this purpose, often disguising the true destinations of these flights by filing "dummy" flight plans. International law, which does not recognize the concept of "rendition," does provide for the compulsory transfer of individuals from one state to another through deportation or extradition with the corresponding judicial procedures and legal remedies.

Interviews with numerous victims of CIA extraordinary rendition flights have revealed how this practice was carried out: Targeted individuals were abducted by CIA agents or the U.S. military (for example in Sarajevo) or were arrested by national security forces and turned over to the CIA (in Sweden, Italy, or Macedonia). Specially trained CIA units, masked and clad in black, cut the clothes off the victims; outfitted them in a diaper and a hooded jumpsuit, opaque goggles, and headphones; strapped them to the floor of the aircraft, often in painful stress positions; and transported them in this condition without food or drink often for hours or even days, to various destinations.

They were taken either to a secret CIA black site (in places like Thailand, Afghanistan, Poland, Romania, or Lithuania) or to a U.S. military prison (such as Guantanamo Bay in Cuba or Bagram in Afghanistan), or they were transferred to national intelligence services to be interrogated ("detention by proxy" in Egypt, Jordan, Syria, Morocco, Pakistan, and other states).

The torture methods used in these states and in various secret prisons such as the CIA "dark prison" in Afghanistan were in some cases too awful for words. In our UN report on secret detention in the fight against terrorism, which I published along with three other experts in 2010, we identified sixty-six states around the world that used secret detention, many of them cooperating closely with the United States.

CHAPTER 15

====

Torture and Enforced Disappearance

The Latin American dictatorships of the 1970s and 1980s perfected an especially perfidious method of torture and repression of dissidents. Individuals were dragged out of bed in the middle of the night by masked and heavily armed agents, beaten and humiliated in front of their children, transported to a secret location in unmarked vehicles without license plates, severely tortured to extract information from them about other dissidents, and then more often than not they were murdered. When their terrified families tried to find out what had happened to them the following day at the nearest police station or military barracks, they were usually told that their whereabouts were unknown but that they had certainly not been detained by state security forces. In fact, the dirty work of enforced disappearances was often given to private paramilitary organizations working hand in glove with the military, police, and secret service. If the families were lucky, the names of their disappeared relatives appeared on a public list and the authorities even promised to do everything in their power to locate them.

The "Advantages" of Enforced Disappearance

The practice of enforced disappearance is an uncomplicated way for the authorities of a state to escape responsibility for the arrest, detention, torture, and often murder of their victims. They pretend to have no information regarding the fate of the disappeared and can even simulate empathy with relatives. There is no need for justification before courts or international monitoring bodies for the arbitrary detention, accusations of torture which might even be based on medical expert opinions, or for that matter for the murder of dissidents. The authorities had nothing to do with the disappearance—perhaps the husband simply needed to disappear in order to move in with his mistress. Another advantage was that especially brutal torture methods could be used during the secret detention without having to worry about possible physical traces, and victims could be detained for as long as it took for any injuries to heal completely. In the event that the torture had irrevocable consequences, another way of circumventing responsibility was to simply kill and bury victims in mass graves or, as in the case of the "dirty war" during the Argentine military junta, to drop them into the sea from aircraft, often still alive. Finally, the practice of enforced disappearances served to generate a climate of fear and intimidation in the general public. As a precursor, the Nazi's Night and Fog Decree had had some measure of success under Wilhelm Keitel, its architect, who holds the dubious distinction of being the inventor of enforced disappearances.

The Suffering of the Victims

For the disappeared, secret (incommunicado) detention entails extreme torment. Victims are completely cut off from the outside world, can communicate with no one, and cannot expect help from anyone. The torturers make it clear to their powerless and helpless victims that they had better cooperate by surrendering the information sought. The disappeared are at the mercy of their captors and exist in a sort of parallel universe, having been removed from the protective precinct of the law. They live in constant fear of being subjected to even more cruel torment and ultimately murder without their fate ever becoming known or the perpetrators prosecuted.

The Suffering of the Families

For victims' families, the uncertainty is far worse than if their husbands, fathers, mothers, or children had been arrested by identifiable security forces and tortured to death in an actual police station. Even though the news of a loved one who has been tortured to death is devastating, relatives can at least begin the mourning process and initiate a rule of law–based investigation of the torture and murder and demand the prosecution of the perpetrators. The worst part of an enforced disappearance are the inevitable feelings of uncertainty and powerlessness. Is my husband still alive? Where is my daughter? Are my parents being tortured at this very moment? Even when rational arguments would appear to indicate that after so many years chances that their loved one will return are slim, relatives cling to the faintest hopes nonetheless: news from another prisoner who many months ago has seen the disappeared alive or has heard or seen this or that from someone else.

Even after an international fact-finding mission had established that practically all of the Bosnian men who disappeared in Srebrenica in July 1995 had been murdered by the Bosnian-Serb army and buried in mass graves, I met numerous women from Srebrenica who were absolutely certain that their husbands or sons had survived the genocide and were still hiding somewhere. Relatives of the disappeared are unable to return to a normal life, to commence the mourning process, or to begin to deal with the past because the past is uncertain. They lead a life trapped between hope and despair, often for years or decades. The women are not eligible for a widow's pension and may not remarry, the children are not eligible for an orphan's pension and never give up the false hope that their father might one day come home.

For the father, suffering might have ended with his murder two days after he was dragged off, but for his family, unfortunately, the suffering, worry, uncertainty, and despair continue for years or decades. Often, the loss of the main provider means that financial hardship and survival concerns are added to all of the other family concerns. This explains why the mothers and grandmothers of the thirty thousand disappeared in Argentina were still demonstrating decades later on the Plaza de Mayo, every week, for truth and justice. There is no normal life for family members of the disappeared. This especially cruel form of human rights violation makes those left behind no less victims than those who were taken and disappeared.

The Practice of Enforced Disappearances Worldwide

The United Nations Working Group on Enforced Disappearances was set up in 1980 in response to this systematic practice by the military in Chile, Uruguay, Argentina, El Salvador, Guatemala, Colombia, and many other Latin American countries. I served on this team as an expert from the Western group from 1993 to 2001. At the time, the practice of enforced disappearances had expanded from its origins in Latin America to become a global phenomenon. Most of the disappeared on our lists were from Saddam

Hussein's Iraq and Sri Lanka. In the course of a mediation mission to Sri Lanka in 1999, we were able to contribute to the clarification of the fate of more than four thousand persons by convincing the government, after extensive negotiations, to pay families compensation and social benefits (pensions, free tuition for children, etc.). In exchange, the families of many persons who disappeared in 1989 and 1990 agreed to accept death certificates issued by the court.

I was especially disturbed by interviews with disappeared Sahrawis who had been secretly held in very small cages in the middle of the Sahara for more than ten years and had suddenly been released by King Hassan II of Morocco as a result of international pressure. These people thought they would never be released and their families had long given up hope of ever seeing them again. One man had actually shrunk by ten centimeters as a result of being bent over in a cell that was so small he was never able to stand or stretch. When the door to his cage was suddenly opened, he was certain he was about to be killed and even months afterward still could not believe he was free. He had lost more than ten years of his life, had no idea what had transpired during this time in the world outside his cage, and was having enormous difficulties starting over again in a new life without fear and in freedom.

The Disappeared in Former Yugoslavia

At the beginning of 1994, I was appointed United Nations expert to investigate more than twenty thousand disappeared persons in the former Yugoslavia. Politically and emotionally, this was the most challenging and frustrating assignment of my career. The collective hopes of the "mothers of Vukovar" and numerous others including organizations in Croatia were pinned on my posting: They were searching for Croatian family members who had disappeared in connection with the ethnic cleansing that had been carried out in Croatia in 1991 by the Yugoslav National Army, along with Serbian militias such as the one headed by the notorious "Arkan" in East Slavonia and other parts of areas controlled by Serbian rebels. Through negotiations and prisoner exchanges we found only very few of these people alive. Others were identified after the exhumations of mass graves such as the one in Ovcara near Vukovar.

The situation in Bosnia and Herzegovina turned out to be more complicated. During the war I was searching along with a small team for disappeared persons in the vicinity of infamous concentration camps such as "Omarska" in northwest Bosnia. Here too our tough negotiations with the three Bosnian warring parties yielded only very few survivors we could return to their families. During the ethnic cleansing the majority of the disappeared had been killed and buried in mass graves, and of these, we were able to identify approximately 300 in Bosnia and Herzegovina alone.

After the Srebrenica genocide in July 1995, we concentrated our work on this area. I was supported by a sizable EU-financed team from the Ludwig Boltzmann Institute of Human Rights and a Finnish team of forensic experts. However, since the mass graves were located in an area that was still under the control of those responsible for the massacre and enforced disappearances (above all in the Republika Srpska), our exhumation work was severely hampered. It would have been easier to carry out exhumations and identifications of the bodies after the end of the war in December 1995, but we would have required protection from the NATO-led International Implementation Force (IFOR). This protection was ultimately refused for political reasons by U.S. IFOR commanders in Sarajevo, as well as U.S. representatives in the Human Rights Commission in Geneva, who explained that exhumations performed "solely" to elucidate the fate of disappeared persons were far too costly and of little benefit.

Whereas negotiations with the three Bosnian conflicting parties about the exchange of disappeared "prisoners of war" were difficult enough (often Muslim men were captured by Croats or Serbs in order to be exchanged subsequently for Serbian or Croatian soldiers), a macabre element was introduced by the bazaar-like negotiations over bodies. When the chief negotiator on the Croatian side proposed in earnest that in exchange for the body of a disappeared Bosnian he should receive two or three Croatian bodies, I left the negotiating table.

The International Commission on Missing Persons

I was already convinced at the time that negotiations between the three Bosnian conflicting parties without the involvement of higher authorities in Belgrade and Zagreb had little hope for success. I therefore proposed in my report to the United Nations Human Rights Commission in the spring of 1996 that an International Commission on Missing Persons should be established and should be made up of the relevant ministers of Serbia, Croatia, and Bosnia and Herzegovina, as well as high-level representatives of the international community. When the United States yet again turned down my proposal in the Human Rights Commission, I realized that it was better to resign (which I did one year later). Three months later, President Bill Clinton took up my proposal and set up an International Commission on Missing Persons in the former Yugoslavia, presided over by former State Secretary Cyrus Vance and appropriately funded. It still exists today and has made an important contribution to the elucidation of the fate of missing persons primarily by opening up mass graves and exhuming human remains.

I have often wondered what could have prompted the Clinton government to turn down my proposal at the United Nations and then move forward on it under U.S. leadership. Perhaps the CIA agent sent to Sarajevo to torpedo my work, as he once told me confidentially, was right when he explained that after the United States had laboriously achieved the Dayton Peace Agreement in Sarajevo, the United Nations had no place there anymore. Nevertheless, many Bosnians who disappeared during the ethnic cleansing, mostly Muslims, have in the meantime been found and identified through the work of the International Commission on Missing Persons, although numerous relatives of the disappeared are still waiting for a satisfactory answer.

The Convention on Enforced Disappearance

In 2001, I was tasked by the United Nations Human Rights Commission to prepare a report on international legal standards for the protection of disappeared persons in the areas of international criminal law, international humanitarian law, and human rights law; to identify possible gaps in this set of standards; and to respond to the question of whether it was advisable to draft a specific convention on enforced disappearance. In my report I answered the question loudly and clearly in the affirmative, and during the following years I worked as an expert with the working group, chaired by France, which had been set up by the Commission to draft such a convention. In December 2006, the International Convention on the Protection of All Persons from Enforced Disappearances was adopted by the UN General Assembly, and it entered into force in 2010. I am extremely pleased that, in spite of all of the compromises, a number of provisions I had originally proposed have survived. Among them are the recognition of relatives as victims of the enforced disappearance, their "right to the truth" as well as to suitable compensation for the suffering caused.

. . . And the Way It Is Disregarded

The convention also contains the express prohibition of any type of secret detention. As we were working on this convention in the United Nations, which was ultimately adopted by the General Assembly, with the United States and a few other states voting against it, there were a growing number of indications pointing to secret U.S. prisons in their War on Terror. By the time we submitted our joint global study on secret detention in the fight against terror to the Human Rights Council, in the spring of 2010, we had identified sixty-six countries that practiced this method to combat terrorism. This practice, by the United States and many other states, fulfills all of the definitional criteria of enforced disappearances and is a devastating reminder of the days of Latin American military dictatorships. In the meantime, however, the states of the world have undertaken to criminalize enforced disappearances and torture. Their systematic practice has even been prohibited internationally as a crime against humanity. In spite of this, President George W. Bush, in September 2006—three months before the adoption of the Enforced Disappearance Convention—publicly admitted that the "high-level detainees" had been transferred from secret CIA detention to Guantanamo Bay. There was not a single word of apology or even the realization that a serious violation of human rights had been committed. Regrettably, much more time will have to pass before those responsible for torture and enforced disappearances are brought to justice.

PART II

Torture in Individual States

With the exception of Austria, where the description of a torture case is based on public sources and my own assessment of the circumstances, the events that occurred in the states as presented in the following chapters represent what I investigated while on official mission as United Nations special rapporteur on torture from 2005 to 2010. The selection of these eighteen countries from all over the world does not tell us anything about the extent of torture which I expected to find. Quite the contrary, my aim was to come up with the most representative cross-section possible of all countries and cultures in order to be able to draw scientifically based conclusions about the actual extent and causes of torture worldwide. Naturally I was able to visit only states whose governments explicitly invited me in my official capacity and had said they agreed with my working methods. Here again I would like to express my gratitude to these eighteen states for their invitation and cooperation.

The individual countries are discussed in the order in which my missions took place. The description of the conditions of detention and the specific aspects of torture in these countries I felt were especially significant are based on my reports, which have been made public and are available on the website of the United Nations high commissioner for human rights (www.unhchr .org). As an independent expert, it is I and not the United Nations who is responsible for the assessment of the situations in these states.

CHAPTER 16

Georgia: Plea Bargaining as a Substitute for Torture?

Georgia 2005, A Model State?

My first investigation mission, in February 2005, was conducted in Georgia, including the breakaway regions of Abkhazia and South Ossetia. Shortly before, the Rose Revolution had led to the assumption of power by President Mikhail Saakashvili, who at first adhered to a publicly declared human rights policy; he brought in a number of committed young people from civil society and placed them in key positions of power. He and his government were genuinely keen to have the most objective possible evaluation of the torture situation and detention conditions in Georgia as well as in the two breakaway regions. Access and fact-finding were greatly facilitated by the Organization for Security and Cooperation in Europe (OSCE). At the time, the actual team was quite small, consisting of one female interpreter and Safir Syed, my first colleague in the Office of the United Nations High Commissioner for Human Rights in Geneva, who would accompany me on many future missions. Although it was his first mission, he had prepared it remarkably well, and this excellent cooperation would only improve in the years to come. In Abkhazia and South Ossetia but also in Georgia, we found inhuman conditions of detention and clear evidence of torture. Most of the politicians did not even refute these findings, describing them as relics of the Shevardnadze era. Working with President Saakashvili, we drafted a long list of recommendations, many of which were actually implemented relatively swiftly. Among the recommendations were a better criminal provision for torture, the appointment of an independent fact-finding commission to inspect places of detention, a far-reaching overhaul of the police department,

ways and means to curb rampant corruption, and the urgently needed renovation or closure of many obsolete prisons. In later years I would often refer
to Georgia as a model for cooperation and the effective implementation of
my recommendations.

Six Years Later

This satisfactory cooperation with the government of Georgia was also one of
the reasons the Ludwig Boltzmann Institute of Human Rights (BIM) selected
it for inclusion in a follow-up project financed by the European Commission.
The project involved supporting selected countries which I had visited as
special rapporteur on torture through concrete measures to implement my
recommendations. This was the purpose of my follow-up visit to Georgia in
April 2011, this time accompanied by Julia Kozma and Johanna Lober. Julia
Kozma and I have long enjoyed excellent working relations. We have undertaken numerous challenging missions together and she is carrying forth this
responsible work as the Austrian member of the European Committee for
the Prevention of Torture (CPT). Johanna Lober joined our team later and
became fully integrated in short order. She also became a member of an investigation commission of the Human Rights Advisory Council in the Austrian Ministry of the Interior.

A good deal had changed in the meantime: The office of the relatively independent ombuds institution was entrusted with the responsibility of carrying out visits to detainees in preventive custody, the police department was
restructured and corruption had been brought "under control," which it was
generally felt had led to a reduction in the risk of torture. Crime had decreased drastically; many of the obsolete prisons had been replaced by new
facilities, leading to a significant improvement in detention conditions. Only
the criminal investigation of torture complaints and the punishment of perpetrators were still inadequate. We were informed by the Justice Ministry
that my recommendations to combat impunity had indeed been discussed,
but in the end had intentionally not been implemented. This prompted us to
focus our follow-up project on this very issue. We were stunned when the
government informed us shortly after our visit that they were not really interested in curbing impunity of torturers and that, instead, we should consider
investing the EU's project resources in an African country. Evidently,

Saakashvili's government has been so spoiled by projects from the United States, the EU, and the Council of Europe to combat torture that they had self-assertively decided to turn down our proposal to provide advice and cooperation.

Indulgences Trump Judicial Procedures

We were genuinely puzzled upon our closer analysis of developments in the criminal justice system. Whereas on my first visit the prisons were hopelessly overcrowded, with more than seven thousand detainees, in the last six years that number had increased more than threefold. Extensive support from the United States had led to Georgia having one of the highest detention rates in the world, ranked just after the United States and Russia. Was this the price that the country was prepared to pay for an all-out fight against crime and corruption? I was even more taken aback when I analyzed the plea-bargaining statistics, a practice borrowed from the United States in which a guilty plea is entered in exchange for an opportunity to negotiate the sentence with the court. Official figures point to a 0.01 percent acquittal rate in criminal cases and four-fifths of cases settled through plea bargaining, an achievement the government stresses with pride. An attempt to grasp these two statistics simultaneously yields the following conclusion: Regardless of whether or not one is guilty of having committed a crime that one is accused of, plea bargaining is the best way to avoid a lengthy prison sentence. If I do not plead guilty, I have a very low probability of being acquitted even if I am in fact innocent. If I am convicted, I will in all likelihood receive a relatively lengthy sentence. It is therefore clearly in my interest to plead guilty (even if I am innocent), because in so doing there is a high probability, depending on how much I am willing to pay, that I will receive a much shorter prison sentence or simply have to pay a mere fine.

If I extrapolate from this model of a "modern" criminal justice system, it leads me to a possible explanation as to why torture in Georgia has decreased significantly over the last few years. If huge numbers of confessions can be achieved through plea bargaining, because the sentences are very strict and the chances of an acquittal are practically non-existent, then torture as a means of extracting confessions becomes superfluous. In addition, plea bargaining generates a good deal of income for the state and provides relief for overcrowded prisons. Those who are well-off will, after all, spend a pretty penny to convert a prison sentence into a mere fine. On the surface, plea bargaining serves everyone, except the poor. Whether this class justice tool is compatible with European principles of rule of law, democracy, and human rights is another matter.

CHAPTER 17

Mongolia: Death Penalty as a State Secret

Unspeakable Detention Conditions

My visit to Mongolia in June 2005 revealed that places of detention were rife with a high level of violence as well as brutal torture methods. This time, along with Safir Syed, I had a British BIM staffer with me, Elizabeth McArthur, with whom I had written an extensive academic commentary on the United Nations Convention against Torture. Two detainees had been tortured to death immediately before our visit. As was the case in other socialist and former Soviet republics, we were appalled at the cruel and retribution- (as opposed to rehabilitation-) based penal/prison system.

In addition to deprivation of personal liberty, detainees who had received lengthy prison sentences were the subject of targeted bullying as per a special regime. They were being harassed and victimized not because they were deemed to be violent or dangerous or had violated prison rules but because such harsh measures, above and beyond their prison terms, had been imposed at the time of sentencing. This aggravated punishment could not be lifted even for good behavior. Detainees who had been sentenced to thirty years for serious crimes had to serve this time, on account of this aggravated punishment regime, in permanent solitary confinement. They were allowed visits by relatives only twice a year and had to have their hands and feet bound during these visits. We interviewed nine of these long-term detainees in their dismal cells, all in a row, in maximum security prison 405 ("Takhir Soyot") and it was immediately clear to us that they were all mentally ill and some physically ill as well. The long periods of solitary confinement had broken them. Some felt that the death penalty would have been more humane than this form of confinement. Twice a week they were allowed one hour outside their cells (if it was not unbearably cold) but were handcuffed and isolated from their fellow detainees during this time. There were no sports, and no self-improvement or work opportunities or activities for these suffering people to while away their time and prepare them for some sort of life after prison. These detainees had not been offered any of the rehabilitation and reintegration opportunities that are goals of any modern penal justice system and that states have committed to abiding by under international law through the International Covenant on Civil and Political Rights. Tears streaming down his face, a detainee told me that he had asked his children not to visit him anymore because the rare and brief visits, now long in the past, were too painful for him and too humiliating because his hands and feet were bound during the visits.

The Inhuman Treatment of Detainees on Death Row

The situation of those on death row was even more horrific. Prisoners' time on death row before their execution, which was usually several months, was spent not only in complete isolation but in the dark with hands and feet bound. During this time they were allowed one single visit from a relative. If a death row inmate was married and had children, he had to decide whether he wished to say farewell to his wife or to one of his children.

The circumstances surrounding the death penalty in Mongolia were considered a state secret, as was the case in some of the other socialist or former Soviet republics. Although when I was invited by the government I was assured of their full cooperation, that any information I required would be provided, and that I would have access to any detainee I wished to interview, in fact neither the minister of justice, the chief public prosecutor, nor a Supreme Court judge would tell me how many detainees had received the death penalty or how many had been executed. It was explained to me that this information was a state secret and could only be revealed by the president. When I put the question to the president of the republic, Natsagiin Bagabandi, at the end of my mission, he replied with a friendly but determined expression that he would be committing a crime if he were to divulge this state secret.

In a case involving an individual complaint against Belarus, in which the situation was comparable, the UN Human Rights Committee ruled that the aim of keeping secret the circumstances of an execution was to intimidate, punish, and intentionally cause family members to feel uncertainty and despair and was to be considered inhuman treatment.

In my report on Mongolia I endorsed this legal opinion and furthermore qualified the detention conditions on death row as torture. I called on the government to abolish aggravated punishment for detainees with lengthy sentences and those on death row, to put a stop to the secrecy surrounding the death penalty, and to purely and simply abolish capital punishment. Even though the government at first did not respond to my request, I was very pleased when a moratorium on the death penalty was announced on 14 January 2010 and when capital punishment was finally abolished on 3 December 2015. It is high time for other socialist and former Soviet republics such as China or Belarus to make this archaic form of punishment a thing of the past.

CHAPTER 18

Nepal: "A Little Bit of Torture Helps"

Systematic Torture

My arrival for a visit in the Kingdom of Nepal in September 2005 accompanied by Julia Kozma and Safir Syed coincided with the peak in the armed conflict between the king and the Maoists. Parliament had been dissolved and political parties were banned. A fairly significant part of the country was under the control of the Maoists, and the security situation was extremely tense. Nepal was one of only two states (along with Equatorial Guinea) where we established that systematic torture was taking place, with the Police, the Armed Police, and the Royal Nepalese Army, in addition to the Maoists, as perpetrators. Extremely brutal methods were used to extract confessions but also to gain information of an intelligence or security nature.

Systematic torture is the most serious reproach I could make against a government. It signifies that the use of torture is not only a routine and widespread practice but that it is also explicitly prescribed or at least tolerated by a government. Evidence of systematic torture is very difficult to produce because torture is officially prohibited in every country and no government will admit to ordering torture or even tolerating it. Our approach consisted of supplementing the testimony from torture victims in detention and the expert assessments from our two Nepalese forensic experts with testimony from senior representatives of the security forces, which we managed to achieve through targeted provocation.

Torture Methods

Police headquarters in the old center of Kathmandu is known as "Hanuman Dhoka," a sizable and old building visible from afar and generally feared. The lower levels of the building contain the overcrowded cells, where detainees were held for many weeks at a time. In some cases detainees remained there for many months because of the anti-terrorist laws, their only possessions being the clothes they were wearing.

Detainees were sitting on the bare concrete floor and slept in shifts because there was not enough room for all of them to sleep at the same time. The torture took place on the top floor: detainees were suspended upside down from bamboo poles, hands and feet bound and blindfolded. They were sometimes held in this position for several hours and were beaten with bamboo poles all over the body and especially on the soles of their feet. Some were abused with water torture, others with electric shocks. The other floors of the building contained the offices for the police.

Accusations Denied

We began our inspection on the top floor with a visit to the torture facilities, where no interrogations were taking place at the time. Next we conducted a large number of interviews in the cells with detainees who agreed to talk to us and who described in great detail how they had been tortured on the top floor. We asked them to describe the torture chambers in great detail and then inspected them a second time. Some of the torture instruments, such as the bamboo poles, had been left in the room and we photographed them. Those among the detainees who were willing to undergo a medical examination were examined by our forensic experts. In most of the cases the experts confirmed that the testimony was consistent with the visible traces of torture. We also took photographs of these traces when detainees allowed us to and we swiftly uploaded them to one of our laptops and organized them.

We then had a follow-up meeting with the chief of police and his two deputies. We began the discussion in our usual style, thanking them for their excellent cooperation, and we immediately asked how many cases of torture they had been faced with in the last few months. Torture? Absolutely none, was the reply. If any torture had taken place in this building, then they would be the first to have heard. Should they however hear of a case, then the perpe-trator would be punished with the full force of the law.

At this point we told them all about the cases that had come to our atten-tion in the last few hours. Nothing but lies, they retorted, just to tarnish the image of the police and to evade their proper punishment. We should not believe a word these criminals and Maoists were saying. I asked our forensic expert to report on his findings. Since he was a Nepalese medical doctor and one of the deputies appeared to know him, they all became increasingly ner-vous. The expert explained that he had observed wounds on the bodies of the examined detainees that were entirely consistent with their complaints of torture. Seemingly agitated and insecure, the police retorted that we should not attach any significance to what we had seen because the wounds were ei-ther self-inflicted or had been inflicted by other detainees in an arrangement meant to discredit the police.

Out popped our laptop and we showed them a few carefully selected pho-tos. The effect was devastating. First, the second highest ranking police offi-cer of the state conceded that it was in fact not true that all detainees were tortured, but that if they lied too tenaciously and were too adamant in their rejection of the charges against them, then they just needed a little nudge to act reasonably. "A little bit of torture helps," he said, and we took note of this carefully. I looked at the chief of police and his second deputy, and they looked sheepish but said nothing. I asked if they could corroborate what had just been said. The second deputy nodded, followed by the chief, who also nodded. But we shouldn't think for a minute that all of the detainees were tortured. Only the ones who lied.

A Risky Encounter

We had a similar albeit somewhat riskier encounter a few days later, in the Kohalpur barracks of the Royal Nepalese Army near Nepalganj in the west-ern lowlands. We first inspected the rooms where detainees had been held until very recently, according to our information. We found traces of blood on the walls. We then sat down with the commanding officer in the cool shade of a tree for a discussion. He recounted proudly his time as part of the United Nations Peacekeeping Forces. He knew the United Nations well and had the highest esteem for it. We were interested in knowing how many de-tainees had been held in these barracks over the last few months. Not a single one, was the reply, as there were no cells in the barracks. But we spoke with people yesterday who told us they had been held and beaten in that room over there—I pointed to the one with blood on the walls. A bold-faced lie, the commander replied, because nobody is ever held here. We produced a picture and gave him a name which seemed to jar his memory, and he recalled a Maoist who had been brought in by a special police unit with the exceptional request that they should hold him for a couple of hours until he could be turned over to the regular police. I repeated that the man insisted he had been held and beaten for two days and two nights in that room. Rubbish! The man had confessed to being a Maoist immediately and was therefore not beaten. Only the liars were beaten, he asserted, as he plunged into a tangle of contradictions not even he seemed to notice. The soldiers, who had been eavesdropping on what began as a calm exchange, slowly withdrew. I wanted to know how he was able to determine that someone was lying to him. He knew for sure thanks to his long years of experience as a United Nations peacekeeper and officer. After all, it was easy to tell if someone was lying. Although Julia Kozma quietly started insisting that we wrap up business so that we could depart in one piece, I could not help but point out to him that he had just lied to me but I had not noticed it immediately. He sprang up and shouted that as a former UN officer he refused to tolerate such insults and that there would be consequences for me as a result of my behavior. Julia Kozma and Safir Syed quickly packed up our things and we left the barracks before he could deliver on the consequences he was planning for me. For the first time, a senior army officer had admitted that he had detained and interrogated Maoists in his barracks, something that had always been denied by the army. The blood stains on the walls were evidence of the fact that such interrogations do not always take place without violence.

This occurred in 2005. More than ten years later, in June 2016, I was invited by the British Crown Prosecution Service as expert witness to give testimony before a jury at the famous Old Bailey Criminal Court in London in a universal jurisdiction case against another high-level officer of the Royal Nepalese Army, Lieutenant Colonel Kumar Lama, who was accused of torture in Nepal during the emergency period of 2005. However, despite overwhelming evidence, on 6 September 2016 he was acquitted of all charges.

CHAPTER 19

China: Rehabilitation, Reeducation, or Brainwashing?

A Challenging Mission

The planning and preparation for my mission to the People's Republic of China was the most difficult of them all. Both of my predecessors had invested almost ten years in vain, in an attempt to secure an invitation for a fact-finding mission with a guarantee that our working methods would be respected. Immediately after I was appointed, I pursued this issue and to my surprise I soon had an agreement with the government. I was not an unknown entity for the Chinese foreign ministry because I had been to China a number of times in connection with the EU-China Human Rights Dialogue, and two of my books had been translated into Chinese by the Academy of Sciences of China.

I did make certain concessions, which I did not grant to any other government. I did not budge from my right to full and unfettered access to any place of detention of my choosing and the conduct of confidential interviews with any detainees I selected. In principle, the visits were also unannounced, but I was obliged to allow foreign ministry officials to accompany me during the visits. Although the officials wanted to know which facilities we intended to visit a full day ahead of time, we did not reveal where we were going until the moment we set off in the direction of a prison, a police station, or a reeducation through labor camp. If the journey took an hour, then the authorities had an hour to prepare for our visit and, potentially, hide detainees.

Strictly speaking then, our visits were not unannounced, but I believed this was a small price to pay for the opportunity to conduct the fact-finding mission at all. The fact that in the end we were not allowed to use our still and video cameras in closed facilities, which we had not agreed to before we began the mission and which naturally made our evidence-gathering and documentation much more difficult, was not enough of a reason to call off the mission which had already begun. When the intelligence services began to seriously obstruct our work, I threatened to cancel our mission, a move on my part aimed at reducing to a tolerable level the constant surveillance of our activities.

In spite of these limitations imposed on our investigation potential, our mission in November and December 2005 was deemed successful to the extent that the facts established were sufficient in my view to produce a scientifically based evaluation of the torture situation and conditions of detention in this vast country. Our team for this mission was larger. Along with Safir Syed, the BIM researchers Elizabeth McArthur, and Naoimh Hughes, we were accompanied by Stephanie Kleine-Ahlbrandt, a China expert from OHCHR. We came to the conclusion that although the extent of torture had decreased in regular criminal proceedings over the course of the last few years and particularly in cities, it still had to be qualified as very widespread. This assessment was in principle confirmed by Chinese academics and to a certain extent also by official sources, including Chinese courts.

We focused on the repression of political dissidents, such as members of Falun-Gong, democracy and human rights movement activists, outspoken journalists, and members of the Tibetan and Uighur minorities in the Autonomous Regions of Tibet and Xinjiang. This meant we had to conduct visits to a "reeducation through labor" camp with numerous Falun-Gong member detainees and to prisons where political prisoners with long sentences were held. These included Prison Number 2 in Beijing, the notorious Drapchi and Qushui prisons near Lhasa, and several prisons in Urumqi.

Afraid to Talk to Us

We faced the same situation everywhere. For one thing it was not easy to find detainees who were prepared to speak with us at all. I remember a well-known female Falun-Gong activist, for whom both my predecessor and I had already engaged the "urgent appeals" procedure as she had allegedly been severely tortured. We wanted to check this allegation through our own investigation on the ground. It was difficult to find her because detainees in the reeducation camps are frequently moved around. We finally located her in a

camp near Beijing, doing daily chores with other women. I introduced myself
and asked if she would agree to be interviewed confidentially. She looked at
me, began to cry as she thanked me for coming, but firmly turned down my
request, stating that she only had a little over a year to serve in this reeducation camp. She was certain that an interview with me would mean several
additional years in the camp, which she would probably not survive.

Liu Dao Wan is a notorious remand prison in Urumqi where the female
Uiguhr leader Rebiya Kadeer has been held in incommunicado detention
and tortured between 1999 and 2001. The detainees in that prison, who spent
most of the day in their cells in a cross-legged posture memorizing the Chinese criminal code, did not even dare look up at us when I asked if they
would agree to be interviewed individually. Even the officials from the foreign ministry were embarrassed by their fear of speaking with us and tried
repeatedly to reassure the detainees, explaining that an interview with me
would not lead to any reprisals.

After trying unsuccessfully in nine cells with thirty detainees each, we
found a detainee from Malawi in the tenth cell who jumped at the chance to
talk with us in English. He did not speak a word of Chinese and was bored
to tears memorizing the criminal code from dawn to dusk every day. Although the prison staff did their best to convince me that the detainees were
shy and disciplined only because of my presence and that their daily routine
was completely different, this detainee informed me that since his transfer
to this facility more than a month before, his as well as the others' sole activ-
ity had been these mindless reeducation methods. Worse still was the fact
that this was a remand prison, and that these detainees, who had not even
been convicted yet, were already being reeducated. This detainee wanted to
know whether his situation was inconsistent with the principle of the presumption of innocence, to which I responded that he was right but that,
unfortunately, this principle did not apply in China. A Falun-Gong member,
for example, could still be sent to a reeducation camp for three to four years
for counterrevolutionary or anti-social activities without even coming close
to a courthouse.

Brainwashing

Even in Drapchi, the well-known prison in the Autonomous Region of Tibet,
it was very difficult to find any detainees who were willing to risk talking to

us. Those who did ultimately muster the courage to do so insisted on absolute confidentiality. The prison director was extremely proud to inform us that all of his detainees, in the end, had confessed and realized the evil of their ways. Many Tibetans who were accused of counterrevolutionary activities or of advocating separatism, in particular monks and nuns belonging to the "Dalai Lama Clique," had claimed their innocence at the trial but had nonetheless been sentenced to lengthy prison terms. They had acknowledged their guilt over the years thanks to the prison's reeducation system. Only those who confessed in prison and accepted that their offense was wrong could enjoy such benefits as sports or other activities to help pass the time, or even be granted an early release.

I was especially shocked by a brief exchange I had with a nun who had been convicted and sentenced to a fifteen-year prison sentence for hoisting, along with her husband who was a Lama, a Tibetan flag in Lhasa in 1999. They had both claimed their innocence at their trial and at the same time admitted they were followers of the Dalai Lama and were prepared to continue to fight for the rights of Tibetans and increased autonomy.

As I began to ask her about these events in her past, she looked at me with sad and forlorn eyes and explained she did not wish to remember. She had simply given up due to the constant reeducation pressure and accepted that it had been misguided to have fought for the freedom of Tibetans. I should stop asking her questions because she no longer wished to face the past. She turned away and went back to work on a loom with other women. Her will was clearly broken and she seemed to have found a certain inner peace.

The director explained later that thanks to the successful reeducation strategy, her sentence had been reduced from fifteen to thirteen years. I asked him if he was clear about the difference between reeducation and brainwashing and his response was that I evidently did not understand the Chinese mentality.

Political prisoners in Drapchi who refused to accept guilt and wrongdoing in spite of the relentless brainwashing were transferred in April 2005 to the new Qushui prison which the Chinese authorities tried hard to conceal from us. We discovered that this prison existed as a result of intensive investigations in Drapchi. We had a good deal of trouble arranging a visit to this new place of detention and it required a threat to break off our mission if we were not taken there. All of the monks imprisoned in Qushui had received long sentences and were unanimous in reporting the conditions of detention in this modern prison as far worse than in Drapchi. Many were allowed a maximum of only twenty minutes per day outside their cells, were not allowed to pray, read, or do anything else that was meaningful, and suffered from the poor quality of the food, the extreme temperatures, and the hopelessness of their situation.

My impression of the majority of detainees here was that in much the same way as in Prison Number 2 in Beijing, the most important prison for political prisoners, it would not be long before their inner resistance, their free will, was broken. Chinese-style rehabilitation?

CHAPTER 20

Jordan: General Intelligence as a Cradle of Torture

Jordan is the only state in the Arab region that invited me to visit and accepted my fact-finding methods. This was surprising given that the General Intelligence Directorate (GID) and the Criminal Investigation Department (CID) routinely and brutally tortured. The Jordanian government deserves to be commended for this invitation, in contrast with other torturing states in the region who turned down my repeated requests for a visit (Algeria, Egypt, Syria, Saudi Arabia, and Iran as a non-Arab state). Jordan also happened to be one of the closest allies of the Bush administration in the War on Terror and made available to the CIA a secret detention center and torture facility in the headquarters of the GID.

The Nerve Center of the Jordanian Intelligence Service

The General Intelligence Directorate headquarters, not unlike a modern fortress, sits on a hill on the outskirts of Amman with a view of the city. Already on the second day of my mission in June 2006, we dropped in unannounced on the GID. Our seasoned team this time was made up of Julia Kozma, Safir Syed, and Derrick Pounder, a noted and experienced forensic doctor from Scotland. The intelligence officers, clearly reluctantly, had to admit us into their well-guarded fortress because I had a letter of authorization issued by the highest government authority. We also inspected the detention center, where individual cells are arranged in a circle, as well as the notorious interrogation rooms where detainees were often mistreated and tortured for hours at a time. The falanga method was used, which means the soles of their feet were beaten, and afterward they were forced to walk on salt, which made the pain almost unbearable and at the same time caused the wounds to heal more quickly along with the traces of torture.

A few days after this visit we went to the Juweidah women's prison, where we interviewed Sajida Mubarak Atrous, the Iraqi woman who was arrested in connection with the infamous November 2005 suicide bombings of hotels in Amman in which more than sixty people were killed. She received the death penalty in September 2006 and was later executed. She told us in detail how she had been tortured every day for a month by Colonel Ali B., the head of the counterterrorism unit, and his staff at the GID headquarters. Her body was completely black from the beatings, and this was apparently also corroborated by staff of the Red Cross, who visited her at the prison.

The Omnipotent Intelligence Service

The colonel was readily identifiable on account of his small size and unmistakable red hair. During our visit to the GID I had taken a photograph of him which I later showed to Sajida Mubarak Atrous. She identified him immediately as her main torturer, as did many other detainees in various prisons with whom we had discussed their experience at the GID headquarters. When we were about to begin our interviews with the GID detainees, the colonel insisted on having a soldier present during our interviews to protect us. We once again produced our letter of authorization, which stated unmistakably that the interviews were to be confidential. Regardless, he insisted on this condition, which we naturally could not accept. A call to his superior was not able to clear up the matter, so we had to leave the GID headquarters, protesting this flagrant violation of my working methods and the assurance from the Jordanian government that my methods would be respected. We were still not able to make any progress on this issue when we brought it up a number of times with the Foreign Ministry over the course of the next few days. This is clear proof of how powerful the GID is in Jordan.

The colonel had good reasons to prevent confidential interviews with the detainees. The torture methods used, according to the testimony of numerous detainees we interviewed in several prisons, included various hanging methods (Palestinian hanging, chicken, ghost position, etc.) and were among the most cruel I had ever encountered in my investigations. Moreover, at the time, one floor of the GID headquarters building must still have been in operation as a CIA secret prison, as was later confirmed to me by a reliable source in connection with our global study on secret detention in the fight against terrorism. Had we been granted confidential interviews with detainees, we most likely would have gleaned information about the location of this secret prison.

Awkward Lies

Further proof of the omnipotence of the GID was the government's reaction to the well-known case of the Canadian Syrian dual national Maher Arar, who was arrested by the United States in New York in September 2002. He was then shipped off to Syria via Amman on a CIA extraordinary rendition flight, where he was severely tortured and then released at the request of the Canadian government. After a detailed investigation by an independent Canadian commission, he received compensation from the Canadian government amounting to 10.5 million Canadian dollars.

This investigation revealed with certainty that Maher Arar was picked up by the Jordanian Intelligence Service on 9 October 2002, upon arrival in Amman on a private plane chartered by the CIA. He was then taken, blindfolded, to a detention center (presumably the GID headquarters), interrogated, and then taken, again blindfolded, to the Syrian border by car. In spite of these findings, the colonel and the deputy director of the GID maintained, when I unexpectedly asked them about this case, that Maher Arar had landed in Amman as an ordinary passenger on a regular Royal Jordanian Airlines flight, but had been stopped and prevented from entering the country because his name was on a list of terrorists. Since no convenient connecting flights were available that day, Maher had asked the officials to be so kind as to take him to Syria. The friendly GID agents could not resist helping a wanted terrorist and they drove him to the Syrian border. He was therefore never arrested, according to their story.

Although this story was hard to believe and had evidently been made up in haste because of my sudden surprise question, and had caused astonishment and anger in Canada and Syria, the government did not dare contradict the testimony of the two GID agents, neither during our concluding debrief at the end of the mission nor later when we showed them our provisional and still confidential report. I had no other choice but to include in my report this much ridiculed version as the official Jordanian position.

Criminal Police Headquarters in Amman

The cruelty of Jordanian torture techniques was not limited to the Intelligence Services. In Al-Jafr, a remote prison in the desert, we asked the detainees to remove their shirts. With very few exceptions, all of the detainees had serious injuries on their backs as a result of systematic beatings and lashings, as Derrick Pounder was able to establish. In my report I demanded that this prison be shut down, a request to which the government complied in 2006.

On the evening of 28 June 2006, we made an unannounced visit to the Criminal Police headquarters in Amman. A fairly long time passed before we were able to gain entry to the cells in the basement. During our quarter-hour wait outside the entrance to the cells, we could hear a good deal of commotion inside. The staff were obviously moving injured detainees out of their cells and trying to get rid of other evidence of torture. In the meantime, the director of the Criminal Police had been summoned and had arrived in a rush and, embarrassed that we had had to wait so long, presently began to shout at his staff, demanding that they open the door immediately.

The cells were almost empty. One of the detainees was so weak that they had been unable to move him out of sight. He had been so severely tortured just before our visit by "Palestinian hanging" and "falanga" that he had a dislocated shoulder and could not move his arms or walk. We heard from another inmate who had been left behind that that detainee later had to be dragged back to his cell by two fellow detainees.

Following a forensic examination in the cell, we spoke with three of the most senior officers a couple of floors above the torture chambers. It was past midnight but all of the concerned officials had come to speak with us. Naturally, they had never heard anything about torture and simply denied our assertions. We invited them to accompany us downstairs, but when we reached the basement, the tortured detainee was no longer in his cell. Apparently, Colonel Assad B., the director of the Criminal Police, had had him removed while we were upstairs with the three police officers.

By this point I had had enough of the lies and hide and seek games they were playing. Through enormous pressure on our side, we managed to get the authorities to produce the torture victim the following morning. In the presence of Derrick Pounder, two medical doctors from the National Institute for Forensic Medicine conducted a thorough forensic examination on the victim. All three experts were unanimous in their assessment that his injuries could only have been caused by the torture methods the victim had described.

Although I requested that criminal charges be brought against the three officers for complicity in the perpetration of the crime of torture, in the end only the actual torturers were punished, not for torture but for disobedience.

The Government's Readiness to Cooperate

While the forensic examinations were being carried out, I was already involved in a concluding discussion with the foreign minister and other senior members of the Jordanian government. We reported our findings to them with respect to the extent and methods of torture in their country. We also informed them that the GID and CID had attempted numerous times to hinder our investigation, had lied to us, and had attempted to conceal torture. Our report was noted without comment.

After this official meeting, Foreign Minister Abdelelah Al-Khatib asked to meet privately with me. With surprising openness, he thanked me for my visit to his country and observed that in his view, all of my findings and conclusions were accurate and he would do everything in his power to implement my recommendations. His only request was that I try to avoid an extremely critical discussion in the media. This was going to be difficult, since all of my reports are public United Nations documents and I had already arranged a press conference in Amman, which was standard procedure for all of our missions. I did do my best to stress to the media that I had had the full cooperation of the government. Notwithstanding, the embarrassing Maher-Arar case and other lies from the GID side I was obliged to include in my report did damage Jordan's standing in the world. The Jordanian ambassador in Geneva was so angry that he did his utmost to torpedo the renewal of my term by the Human Rights Council in 2007.

CHAPTER 21

Austria: The Case of Bakary Jassey

I was on holiday with my family in Austria in April 2006 during Easter week when I received a telephone call from Martin Kreutner, head of the then Bureau for Internal Affairs (BIA) of the Austrian Federal Ministry of the Interior. This unit, which was directly under the minister (at the time Liese Prokop) but otherwise free from directives and external influence, was responsible for cases of serious accusations against the police anywhere in Austria, especially for the investigation of accusations of corruption and mistreatment. Kreutner is an expert in the fight against corruption and has become adept at dealing with difficult police investigations of accusations of mistreatment by police officers. This task is all the more challenging because the esprit de corps unfortunately is still widespread within the Austrian security forces. If accusations are leveled against colleagues, the police in Austria behave no differently than what we have observed in countries that torture on a daily basis: stick together, lie, block external investigations, implement reprisals and legal countermeasures against those who allege they have been tortured or mistreated. The legal measures run the gamut from defamation lawsuits to resisting public authority.

The Human Rights Advisory Council and Its Commissions as Part of the Ministry of the Interior

After the death by suffocation of the Nigerian Marcus Omofuma, whose mouth was taped shut so that his screaming would not inconvenience the other passengers too much while he was being deported by plane in 1999, the Human Rights Advisory Council (MRB), along with six independent investigation commissions and the BIA, were created, all under the Ministry of the Interior. I was appointed chairperson of Commission 2, with jurisdiction in the northern part of Lower Austria (Weinviertel and Waldviertel) as well as Vienna districts 1, 2, 20, 21, and 22, including the well-known police prison located on Rossauer Lände. The commissions were made up of seven members from different professions, including medicine, psychology, social work and law.

We carried out unannounced visits and confidential interviews with detainees in all places of detention that are under the responsibility of the Ministry of the Interior, from individual cells in a small police station on the Czech border to large facilities such as the one on the Rossauer Lände in Vienna. In addition, we were allowed to accompany and observe the police during the exercise of direct orders and coercive measures, such as interventions during demonstrations, raids, or expulsions. Awareness and prevention of ill-treatment by the police during arrests or interrogation by the criminal police were of course at the center of our work.

As we had no investigative powers, early on we contacted the BIA, the newly set up special unit housed in the former Meidling barracks. We were impressed from the start by Martin Kreutner's tact and professionalism. He seemed to agree with us that there were far more incidences of ill-treatment by the Austrian police force than generally admitted. His investigation had run into a wall of silence and concealment, as had ours. We decided to exchange information and cooperate in the investigation of abuse. This is the background to our phone conversation in 2006.

During the call he said that the accusations by Bakary Jassey, a Gambian national, might well be true. Jassey had stated that police officers belonging to the Vienna WEGA special forces unit had threatened to kill him and had tortured him severely in an abandoned warehouse in Vienna's second district near the Prater amusement park. Martin Kreutner asked if we could pay Jassey a visit where he was being held in pre-deportation custody at the police detention center, or PAZ (the new name for the former police prison) located on the Hernalser Gürtel. He had ended up there after an interrupted attempt to expel him to Gambia on 7 April 2006.

On the Wednesday following Easter, 19 April 2006, I visited Jassey at the PAZ on Hernalser Gürtel accompanied by Alfred Zauner, Marijana Grandits, and Bettina Frisslovics from Commission 2. He looked dreadful: badly swollen eyes and injuries of the mouth and jaw. He had difficulties moving his head and complained of severe pain. He was extremely wary when he first met us and it took a good deal of convincing before he agreed to be interviewed. What had happened to him?

Due to my official obligation of confidentiality, the following account consists exclusively of facts already made public by the MRB, the media, and NGOs, as well as those reported during the trial. The overall assessment of these facts is my own personal view.

The Attempted Expulsion

Bakary Jassey had been living in Austria for many years and since 2000 had been married to Michaela Jassey, an Austrian national. They have two children, Marcel (born in August 1999) and Amina (born in July 2002). In April 2004, he received a two-year sentence for drug possession with intent to sell, which he served in the Hirtenberg prison. On 31 March 2006 he was released. Jassey's wife Michaela and their two children were waiting for him at the prison gate but were unable to greet him because he was immediately whisked away in handcuffs to the PAZ on Hernalser Gürtel by the Immigration Police, where his expulsion to Gambia had already been arranged. On 7 April 2006, WEGA officers dragged him out of bed at four in the morning without warning and took him directly to Vienna's Schwechat airport. As he boarded a Brussels Airlines aircraft, he told the flight attendant that he had not been informed about this trip, and that he had a spouse and two children in Vienna who had not been informed either. He refused to travel on the aircraft, whereupon the co-pilot announced that he would not allow Bakary Jassey on board.

Torture in the Warehouse

On the way back to the PAZ, Jassey's three WEGA team escorts told him that they had been ordered to kill him. After numerous telephone calls with a fourth WEGA agent, who had the keys to an abandoned warehouse on Wehlistrasse adjacent to the Prater park, they took him in a police van to the warehouse, which WEGA used for training purposes. His hands were tied together with a red rope, he was insulted with racist slurs and told that the time had come for his execution. Subsequently, he was severely beaten and kicked by the three policemen, who wore thick black gloves, until he lay motionless on the ground. They then dragged him to the middle of the warehouse and ordered him to kneel, eyes closed, on the concrete floor in a Muslim prayer position. Next, he was hit from the rear by the police van, which caused him to pitch forward and strike his head on the concrete floor, whereupon he lost consciousness in the belief that he had been executed. When he regained consciousness, he was bleeding from his head and nose and had severe pain all over his body. The WEGA agents carried him into the van, placed him on the floor, and drove him to the General Hospital (AKH), where he was taken to the emergency room on a stretcher.

Although Jassey tried to explain to the doctors that he had just barely survived a botched execution with resulting broken bones and other serious injuries and that he feared for his life acutely, the doctors seemed to give more credence to the agents' story, namely that his injuries had been caused by his attempt to flee. The doctors treated his immediate injuries, placed a neck brace on him, and turned him back over to the police despite his pleas to be admitted. None of the medical doctors on duty felt it worthwhile discussing privately with Bakary Jassey his version of the "attempted escape," nor did any of them feel he should undergo a thorough medical examination in view of his accusation of serious abuse. On the way back to the PAZ on Hernalser Gürtel, his torturers removed the neck brace and warned him in no uncertain terms of the serious consequences for him if he told anyone what they had done to him.

Back to the Hernals Police Detention Center

Since the WEGA agents told the PAZ that Jassey had attempted to flee in the 8th district of Vienna on the return trip from the airport and had resisted arrest when he was re-captured, and that the use of force had been unavoidable, he was immediately placed in isolation in a security cell. In addition, he was charged with resisting arrest. In spite of his severe pain and his pleas for help, he received no medical treatment on that day nor was he allowed to make a telephone call.

The next day, finally, on the Saturday after Good Friday, one of the staff members on duty took pity on Jassey and allowed him to make a call to his wife. He reached his mother-in-law and explained to her where he was and that he needed help urgently. She informed her daughter, who rushed to the PAZ with both children. The helpful staff member arranged for them to meet in the visiting room. When the children saw the state he was in they began to scream and were taken out of the room. But Michaela Jassey was alert enough to take photographs with her mobile phone of her husband's battered and swollen face. It is thanks to these two coincidences that this case of torture was satisfactorily investigated and elucidated. Michaela Jassey immediately informed her husband's attorney, Amnesty International, and the media. On 10 April, Heinz Patzelt and Andrea Huber from Amnesty International and Nina Horaczek from the *Falter* weekly began investigating, and on the very next day Bakary Jassey was questioned by agents of the BIA, who also visited the warehouse with him.

It was this visit to the warehouse and the analysis of the data on the mobile phones of the WEGA agents that had prompted Martin Kreutner's aforementioned call.

Another Four Months in Pre-Deportation Detention and Continued Threats of Expulsion

The PAZ staff and the Immigration Police were undeterred by the BIA, Amnesty International, and media investigations. There was no doubt in their minds that Bakary Jassey was a violent detainee who had resisted deportation, had attempted to escape, and had resisted arrest. He was therefore placed in solitary confinement for almost a week: the first few days as a disciplinary measure because of his resistance and the rest of the time as a security measure because he was considered dangerous.

At the request of the BIA, the prosecution began preliminary proceedings against the four agents. Amnesty International, the media, and my commission requested Jassey's immediate release in an urgent appeal to the Human Rights Advisory Council on 28 April 2006. In addition, it was established through a CAT scan ordered by the court that he had fractures of the orbital cavity, upper jaw, and cheekbone. Notwithstanding, Bakary Jassey remained in pre-deportation detention. On 31 May, despite growing pressure from the body of evidence, the Independent Administrative Senate (Unabhängiger Verwaltungssenat, or UVS) of Lower Austria rejected the appeal against his custody pending deportation by his attorney on the grounds that his deportation order was still in effect and that his testimony as a witness in the criminal trial of the four WEGA agents could also be arranged "from outside the country."

This ruling by the UVS with its somewhat bizarre justification was finally lifted on 23 October 2008 by the Administrative Court due to unlawfulness of its content. The Court ruled that the UVS had completely disregarded the fact that the authorities were in possession since 25 April 2006 of "numerous official medical findings and expert opinions which indicated that a deportation of the complainant was impossible, until further notice, on account of these attestations of a post-traumatic stress reaction."

During the ongoing criminal proceedings against the four WEGA officers, the Ministry of the Interior tried repeatedly to deport the principal witness. The Human Rights Advisory Council and its commissions had to take extraordinary measures to prevent this from happening.

On 10 July 2006, Bakary Jassey, still in severe pain, was driven to a psychiatrist in Innsbruck by the Immigration Police with the energetic support of an NGO that calls itself "Austria Human Rights Association." This NGO worked closely with the Ministry of the Interior and was tasked with convincing pre-deportation detainees to "return voluntarily" to their country of origin. The psychiatrist was supposed to contradict her colleagues in Vienna by certifying that he was "deportable." In the end, the Administrative Court put an end to the deportation attempts by the Ministry of the Interior with a preliminary injunction on 25 July 2006 and Bakary Jassey was released from pre-deportation detention four months to the day after being tortured.

The Criminal Trial of the WEGA Agents

The oral hearing in the case against the four WEGA agents took place at the Vienna Regional Criminal Court on 30 and 31 August 2006. The courtroom was so crowded that Heinz Patzelt and I barely managed to find a seat. Many human rights activists, who had waited for a long time outside the courtroom, could not be admitted. It had been quite some time since I had attended a trial and I had long had utter confidence in the independence of the Austrian justice system. My confidence was shaken to the core, however, by the disgraceful show put on for our benefit by the judge over the course of these two days. For almost twenty years I have decried in vain the fact that in Austria, in a blatant violation of the United Nations Convention Against Torture (CAT), the serious crime of torture is not classified as a criminal offense (with appropriate punishment). Austria had not fulfilled this requirement under Article 4 CAT, which the United Nations Committee Against Torture had repeatedly criticized. It was only in reaction to the Jassey case that the Austrian Parliament finally enacted a special crime of torture in 2013. At the time of the verdict, the only act established as a criminal offense was "tormenting and neglecting a detainee" (Section 312 of the criminal code), punishable by an absurdly short sentence of a maximum of two years. However, if the crime is aggravated by serious bodily harm, as in the Jassey case, a conviction could have carried a sentence of up to five years. There was no longer any doubt, after all of the material evidence, in particular the analysis of the mobile telephone surveillance data by the BIA, that the four WEGA agents were guilty.

Whereas up until the oral hearing, the four agents had denied everything, presenting a variety of creative lies, slandering and leveling extremely serious accusations at Bakery Jassey, in fact the mock execution and the torture (physical and mental) had been meticulously planned and carried out with extreme cruelty. But then, suddenly, they confessed in the courtroom. Truth be told, the judge put the words in their mouth: "So you gave him a trouncing, did you?" The defendants silently nodded. No sign of remorse. This was anything but a confession that deserved leniency. Role reversal. Anyone sitting in the courtroom without prior knowledge of the facts would think that the African guy was the defendant and the policemen were the victims. Although he was fluent in German, Bakary Jassey was repeatedly interrupted, intimidated, and rebuked by the judge. A good deal more attention was paid to his past conviction as a "drug dealer" than to the torture he endured in the warehouse. The policemen were depicted as decent family men who had simply overreacted when provoked by this aggressive African man. It was no surprise then that the judgment was lenient: the three torturing policemen were sentenced to eight months on probation, the guard received six months on probation.

While we were discussing, in a state of shock, the blatant discrimination of the trial and the extremely mild sentence, the policemen accepted the sentence and the public prosecutor, who had acted in a clearly restrained fashion during the entire trial, immediately waived his right to appeal. His motive was clear: A conditional conviction of less than a one-year sentence meant that a civil servant does not automatically lose his job. A removal at this point could only be achieved through a disciplinary action, which was unlikely based on my knowledge of the Austrian disciplinary authorities and the role of the staff representative in such an action.

That day, 31 August 2006, I felt ashamed to be Austrian. As the United

Nations special rapporteur on torture, I was working to achieve justice for torture victims in many countries all over the world. And here I sat, observing the way justice was served in my own country. A relatively minor drug offense had landed a respectable black-skinned African in jail with an unconditional two-year sentence, whereas these white-skinned Austrian policemen, who had brutally tortured the man and threatened to kill him, had received a probationary sentence of a few months and had not been dismissed from their law enforcement positions. Oblivious to the unfairness of the verdicts, the prosecutor let slide the opportunity for an appeal and the judgment took legal effect.

The Disciplinary Ruling and Its Lifting by the Administrative Court

As could be expected, the Disciplinary Authority also failed to act responsibly. On 11 September 2007, the Higher Disciplinary Commission of the Federal Chancellery endorsed the decision that the four torturing policemen could remain in their jobs and even reduced the fines they had received, which were on the order of one to five months' salary. In the past I had criticized the levying of fines as punishment for the crime of torture in countries like Jordan, Nigeria, or Nepal. I had to acknowledge that the practice in Austria was not much better.

Once again the Administrative Court intervened. The decision of the Higher Disciplinary Commission was lifted on 18 September 2008 as unlawful, with a substantiation that could not have been clearer: the Higher Disciplinary Commission had disregarded the significant injustice of the act itself and had not considered its brutality, the consequences of which had been serious injury and traumatization. Neither the simulated execution nor the "fact that the perpetrators' infringement of their official duty had evidently been intentional, premeditated and methodically planned" had been taken into account by the Higher Disciplinary Commission. The Disciplinary Commission had incorrectly considered that the confession should lead to leniency in the judgment of the accused policemen because the fact that "the accused changed their assertions in court was a result of the evidence that had come to light at that point. According to the record, the accused at first denied committing the acts, after agreeing among themselves on their stories, and in their first interrogation had testified that the detainee had injured himself during an escape attempt and in the proceedings before the Disciplinary Commission had continued to deny that the detainee had been intentionally run over by a vehicle, in spite of the relevant legally binding assessment by the court. Moreover, the accused had even attempted to qualify individual points of the criminal justice findings in the trial before the authority." Not until the repetition of the disciplinary procedure on 2 November 2009 did the Disciplinary Commission finally decide on the officials' dismissal. The guard was fined but allowed to remain in his job with the police.

Failure of the Political System

I hope that the torture of Bakary Jassey is a unique case in Austria. What shocked me more than the crime of torture and has shaken my confidence in Austria as a rule-of-law state is the way the political system, and in particular the Ministry of the Interior, handled this case. At the outset, the victim's accusation of torture was routinely dismissed and caused the torturing policemen's position to be bolstered. Despite his severe bodily injuries and sharp pain, Bakary Jassey was held four full months in pre-deportation detention instead of being admitted to a hospital simply because the Ministry of the Interior, blatantly disregarding the overwhelming evidence, insisted on pushing through his deportation and, scandalously, was even assisted in this by the Lower Austria UVS! The medical officers failed completely in their duty to examine without delay any accusations of ill-treatment and to give medical care to an injured detainee.

Moreover, the conduct of the medical doctor on duty at the AKH hospital on 7 April 2006 was at the very least questionable. I do not think that I, as an Austrian, would have been treated in such an irresponsible manner as was Bakary Jassey in those circumstances. Many witnesses considered that the trial was replete with racist prejudices and rigged between the judge and the prosecutor. The same belief was held with regard to the disciplinary procedure.

Even after the conviction of the torturing officers, the Ministry of the Interior continued to try to deport Bakary Jassey to Gambia. He and his Austrian family were able to remain in Austria only because of the medical certificates that attested to his traumatized state and his need for medical and psychological rehabilitation, as well as the joint efforts of NGOs, the media, and the Human Rights Advisory Council.

Inhuman Policy for Foreigners

Bakary Jassey's brutal torture as a reprisal for an interrupted deportation attempt is inexcusable and can only be explained through an inhuman atmosphere caused by many years of the extant policy toward foreigners marked by racist and xenophobic fears. The case was only investigated and resolved because of coincidences and the civil courage of a few people: the courageous PAZ officer who out of pity allowed Jassey to call his spouse from his incommunicado detention and arranged for her to visit him; Michaela Jassey for her alertness in taking photos with her mobile phone of her husband's swollen face and sending them to the lawyer, the media, and Amnesty International; the tireless efforts by Heinz Patzelt, Andrea Huber, Nina Horaczek, and other representatives of civil society and the media; the perseverance and resolve of Martin Kreutner and his BIA team in their independent, objective, and effective investigation and the sharing of evidence with the Human Rights Advisory Council and its commissions, despite fierce resistance from the Ministry of the Interior and the Vienna Police; the commitment of numerous members of the Human Rights Advisory Council and its commissions.

The fact that Bakary Jassey was finally freed after four months of predeportation detention is attributable to the Administrative Court and the reengagement of the scandalous disciplinary procedure.

In the meantime, the BIA was dissolved by former minister Maria Fekter and replaced by the Federal Anti-corruption Office, which only deals peripherally with accusations of mistreatment. Martin Kreutner was forced out of his post as incorruptible investigator and is now secretary general of the International Anti-Corruption Academy in Laxenburg. Austria is still lacking a truly independent and effective body, with no links to the police, for the swift and objective investigation of torture and mistreatment accusations.

Toward the end of its mandate, the Human Rights Advisory Council had established a high-level working group with the task of developing an effective and independent mechanism to investigate and prosecute cases of torture and ill-treatment. In fact, we had reached an agreement with the Ministries of Interior and Justice when the Human Rights Advisory Council was dissolved in 2012. It was replaced by a National Preventive Mechanism (NPM) under the authority of the Austrian Ombuds Board established after Austria had ratified the Optional Protocol to the UN Convention against Torture. The NPM has a much broader mandate than the former Human

Rights Advisory Council at the Ministry of Interior. I was again appointed as head of one of six visiting commissions of the NPM for the period 2012 to 2015. But my efforts to establish an independent mechanism for the investigation and prosecution of torture and ill-treatment remained in vain.

In September 2015, the second Universal Periodic Review (UPR) of Austria took place before the UN Human Rights Council in Geneva. Various governments recommended that Austria establish an independent torture investigation mechanism. I had been appointed by the Austrian minister of justice, Wolfgang Brandstetter, as independent expert to assist him in his function as head of the Austrian delegation. I advised him that Austria should accept this recommendation and swiftly establish such a mechanism. But it would appear that the case of Bakary Jassey has so far not yielded any lessons that remediate Austria's current methods for dealing in a professional manner with allegations of torture and ill-treatment.

CHAPTER 22

Paraguay: Excellent Follow-Up

Long before the military had taken control of most Latin American countries in the 1960s and 1970s, Paraguay had become synonymous with repression and torture under the leadership of Alfredo Stroessner, long-term dictator with ancestors from Hof near Nuremberg. After Stroessner's overthrow in 1989, the country began the arduous task of coming to terms with the past and building rule-of-law institutions.

For my mission in November 2006 I had a new lineup of team members, all just as professional as the last, that included Anna Crawford (Geneva), Roland Schmidt (Vienna), Duarte Nuno Vieira, well-known forensic medical expert from Portugal, as well as interpreters Carmen Stefani-Gari and Roger Kaminker. For Roland, Duarte, and Roger, this was the first of many missions marked by excellent cooperation from the start. Roland became one of my closest colleagues on the Anti-torture Team at BIM and I could always count on his counsel and robust assistance in the most difficult of situations.

Corrupt Justice Ministry

We were able to establish widespread use of torture by the police to extract confessions. One of their preferred methods was to place a plastic bag over detainees' heads and then squeeze their testicles until they almost passed out. This method is very effective at producing confessions and leaves no lasting traces. The justice system was corrupt through and through and the conditions of detention were abysmal. Inmates had to pay for every single privilege, including the privilege of being in the prison at all as it provided them with a roof over their heads. Poor detainees who did not have relatives living nearby to provide them with food, drink, medicine, or even a doctor, were totally dependent on fellow inmates to satisfy the most basic needs to survive. In contrast, well-heeled detainees who paid enough could arrange through the prison staff for a different sex worker every night in a "privado" or private room to spice up their dreary confinement.

A German pretrial detainee in the infamous Tacumbú prison in Asuncion gave me a rundown of the "fees" required for the various "privileges." The director of the Villarica prison was so proud of the Catholic chapel in his jail that he wanted to show it to us but had forgotten that, due to the high occupancy rate of the privados, the chapel had been converted into additional privados. He remembered, a little late, as we barged into the chapel, interrupting the inmates' intimacy.

Exemplary Political Willingness to Change

In spite of the critical findings in our report, the government's reaction was very positive, and it was prepared to implement my recommendations. In the meantime there had been a change of government and the new one appeared to attach a good deal more importance to human rights. This is one reason we had selected Paraguay as the first country in our EU-funded follow-up project. Tiphanie Crittin and Moritz Birk, who joined BIM toward the end of my term and swiftly and smoothly integrated into the team, accompanied me in March 2011 on an evaluation mission that involved a consultation with the government and civil society to determine the specific activities we could support in order to implement my recommendations.

Much had already been done. The Supreme Court had prepared an amendment to the Criminal Code to criminalize torture in line with the CAT, which was deliberated in Congress. Moreover, the Congress had adopted an exemplary piece of legislation setting up an independent National Preventive Mechanism (NPM) to monitor on a regular basis all places of detention as well as an independent Public Defender's Office to strengthen access to legal aid. Furthermore, in the relevant ministries (Interior, Justice, and Public Affairs), human rights departments were created and staffed with professional civil servants.

Together with our local project partner, the well-known human rights NGO network CODEHUPY, with whom I already had excellent contacts during my mission in November 2006, we supported the ongoing important reforms in numerous ways. Notably, we ensured— with the invaluable support of Victor Rodriguez Rescia, member of the UN Subcommittee on Prevention of Torture that had visited the country on an official mission in 2009 and 2010—that the law would be adequately implemented by setting up a qualified and adequately composed selection committee and selection procedure as well as advocating for a sufficient budget. Moreover, we strengthened the capacities of the Public Defender's Office in the prevention of torture and supported the establishment of a prison observatory aimed at improving the situation of persons in detention. The project experienced difficult times when President Lugo was ousted in the aftermath of deadly clashes during an eviction of an occupation by landless farmers in Curuguaty. My team participated in a fact-finding mission to investigate these incidents and fortunately we were able to mediate between civil society and the interim government accused of a "parliamentary coup d'état," in order to keep the project implementation going. Thus, it is extremely gratifying to see that the NPM in Paraguay, composed of the most qualified experts, and the independent Public Defender's Office, are now implementing good practices for the prevention of torture in the region, despite changes in the political landscape that today are less favorable toward the fate of detainees.

CHAPTER 23

Nigeria: Notorious Torture Chamber in Lagos

Nigeria, with more than 170 million inhabitants, is the most populous state in Africa and a major power on the continent. Ethnic and religious tensions in this multiethnic country caused the bloody Biafra secession war in the 1960s, and have the potential to stir up regular conflicts, which have been exacerbated by the federal system and the introduction of Islamic sharia in the northern federal states. The fast-paced development fueled by the discovery of oil in the Niger Delta has harmed the country more than it has helped it: Petrodollars meant enormous profits for oil multinationals, a huge gap between rich and poor, one of the highest corruption and crime rates in the world, and irreversible damage to the environment and to the rights of indigenous peoples in the Niger Delta, which opened the way to armed conflict between the then military government and the "Movement for the Emancipation of the Niger Delta" (MEND). Even after the return to a civil and democratic government under President Olusegun Obasanjo, most of these problems remained unresolved despite significant efforts to the contrary.

Corrupt Criminal Justice

Extreme levels of violence, crime, and corruption had practically caused the justice system to collapse. In March 2007, my group for this mission included Safir Syed, Roland Schmidt, Duarte Vieira, and for the first time Isabelle Tschan, a Swiss human rights expert, seconded to me cost-free by the Swiss Foreign Ministry. Tschan was so successful in her work at BIM that she was enticed away to work for the United Nations Development Program on a project to build democracy and human rights in West Africa.

The detention conditions we found were indescribably horrific. On average, prisons were overcrowded by a factor of two to three and filthy, and the potential for violence was very high. The majority of detainees were on remand because the criminal justice system was not functional and detainees were often "forgotten" if they did not have enough money to bribe the police, prosecutors, or judges. Based on documents we were given, we demanded that the government immediately release twenty thousand to twenty-five thousand detainees because they had already spent more time in pretrial detention than the highest custodial sentence they could have received for the crimes they were accused of committing. Some of the detainees on death row with whom we spoke had spent more than twenty years in the overcrowded death row cells.

Shot in the Legs

The police make routine use of torture to extract confessions. Nigeria is notorious for brutal armed robberies. Someone accused of this crime, rightly or wrongly, must be prepared for "special" treatment by the police and justice system. One of the widespread methods involves shooting the legs of the accused at very close range after arrest or during the initial interrogation. The police report will state that the accused was wounded during an attempted escape or in an exchange of fire. Medical forensic experts such as Duarte Vieira can determine accurately the distance and angle from which a shot was fired by examining the bullet wound. If someone has been shot in the leg from above and from a distance of one meter, which we determined had occurred in numerous similar cases, then the assertion by the police that the individual was shot during an escape attempt is not credible. To make matters worse, victims are frequently left without any medical care whatsoever.

The Police Station in Lagos

An especially notorious police station is the Criminal Police headquarters in Lagos's Panti district, where we made a surprise visit on 6 March 2007. Our completely unexpected arrival triggered lengthy discussions with the acting police chief. I had to show him numerous times a "letter of authorization," signed by the police inspector general in Abuja, which spelled out in detail our investigation requirements and listed all of the members of my team. We were finally granted access to the overcrowded cells containing seventy-two men, all of whom were charged with armed robbery. The cells were dark and stuffy and we had some trouble squeezing past detainees to find a place where we could conduct at least semi-confidential interviews out of earshot and visual range of the officers. Although Nigeria also legally limits the time spent in police custody, the persons we interviewed had already been in these overcrowded cells between five months and more than two years, without ever having left them, and with no visits from a lawyer or relative. In most cases their families did not even know where they were being held. One young man who had already been held for more than a year had wounds in both legs that were the result of gunshots from approximately one meter away. In the absence of any medical care he had used a candle to treat the wounds himself. The detainees we spoke to all testified that severe torture took place in a "torture room," and they described its precise location.

The Torture Room

Entering the building where the torture room was supposed to be, we came upon a spacious office filled with agents of the criminal police interrogating suspects and writing reports. According to the description from the detainees, the room in question was located behind this office. However, as soon as we approached one particular door, officers swiftly blocked our way. The message was unequivocal: entrance to this storage room was strictly prohibited. I then asked Roland Schmidt and our Polish UN security officer, Andrzej Chlebowski, to keep an eye on the door to the torture room while I returned to the office of the acting police chief in one of the other buildings in order to obtain his permission to enter the room.

His refusal to cooperate left me no choice but to call the police inspector general in the capital Abuja, Sunday Ehindero. I will never forget the look of submissive anger from the police chief when he received the order from his highest superior to open the door to the torture room. We ran the gauntlet of criminal police officers who could not believe that their chief had given in to my demand.

The sights and stench of this room surpassed our worst fears. Even Duarte Vieira, our Portuguese physician and one of the leading forensic experts, commented that this was the most dreadful place he had ever inspected.

There were 125 people crammed into this extremely hot, humid, and filthy room without a solid roof, who had to sit and sleep on a dirt floor. A hole in the corner was the only toilet. Among these cowering people were three women and several children, the youngest eleven years old. Many said they were hungry and Duarte noted that some showed signs of malnourishment.

Detainees are taken to this room to be interrogated and tortured immediately after arrest. They are not taken to the cells or officially registered until they have made a confession. Several had been in this room for more than two months. Every single person we spoke to had been severely tortured and the torture had taken place in front of the others. When we assured them that we would not allow the authorities to enter the room, one man even demonstrated how he had been suspended just above the floor, in a painful position with hands and feet bound behind his back and to an iron bar, and to make the pain even more excruciating, a part from a car engine had been placed on his back.

On occasion detainees were forced to participate in the torture of others. All of the torture instruments described by the detainees in detail, including the engine part, were in the room, and Duarte was able to document and photograph recent torture wounds on many detainees. He was also able to match the wounds with the torture instruments used: bullet wounds, skin burns by hot machetes, bruises and open wounds caused by beatings with iron bars, wooden sticks, and plastic hoses. All of this torture paraphernalia was neatly hung on the walls. One young man, Bayo Abdur Mohammed Adekunk, whose bullet wounds had been hastily bandaged, complained he was in terrible pain. When Duarte attempted to remove his bandages, we noticed that his foot was completely putrid. We could hardly distinguish between the bandages and the decaying flesh. The pain must have been unbearable for him. For us, the mere sight and stench of this human being's limb were hard to bear.

Indifference Toward Inhumanity

The brutal and inhuman attitude of the staff of this police station vis-à-vis their detainees in the adjoining room was also very hard to bear. Everyone knew that people have been tortured and humiliated here for years, and apparently it never occurred to anyone that something was not right. Torture had become routine, a trivial everyday occurrence, much like other tasks.

Duarte's remark that Bayo Abdur Adekunk's leg, as well as the lower extremities of other detainees we had identified, had to be amputated immediately because otherwise these men would surely die of their infections within a few days simply drew a shrug from the police chief during our final meeting. There were no funds for this sort of thing. Surely we could not expect the police chief to pay out of his own pocket for such expensive hospital bills. It took another telephone call to Inspector General Ehindero to reinforce our demands.

During our last meeting with the inspector general, members of the Nigerian government and President Obasanjo in Abuja, we discussed numerous other problems and individual cases, and we raised the issue of the fate of the detainees in the torture room in Lagos, showing the photos we had taken to our speaking partners. From their reactions, I could easily see who was completely familiar with these barbarities and who was genuinely shocked. Whereas most of the police and military officers did not appear to be particularly surprised, I would say that the politicians and even Inspector General Ehindero must not have actually known about these abhorrent torture practices. President Obasanjo promised that he would personally look into this problem and would see to it that my recommendations were implemented.

At my request, Andrzej Chlebowski and several other United Nations staff who were stationed in Nigeria inspected the police station in Panti a few weeks after our departure and found that the torture room was empty. The fate of the three detainees in Lagos who had received severe gunshot wounds was not clear, although President Obasanjo assured me of his full support at a meeting we had in Vienna in May 2007.

I have been informed that of the twenty thousand to twenty-five thousand pretrial detainees whose immediate release I had demanded, many had likely been freed soon after my departure. But it appears that at least two of the three seriously wounded detainees in the Panti police station in Lagos, namely Bayo Abdur Adekunk and Elijah John, died of their wounds shortly afterward, although they had been swiftly admitted to a hospital. Although Sunday Ehindero's successor, Police Inspector General Mike Okiro, assured me in a letter dated 14 September 2007 that the officers responsible for the torture and deaths had been prosecuted, I have yet to hear of any convictions.

So long as officers who implement torture can count on impunity and a lack of consequences with regard to their actions, effectively combating torture, a routine occurrence, is going to be an uphill battle in this country.

Alongside impunity, the pervasive corruption in the justice sector must be addressed and a human rights culture must become embedded in the mind-set of the police. The two officers who man the human rights desk at the entrance to the cells at the Panti police station, who were doing their jobs and allegedly saw nothing at all, are certainly not fit to ensure that a human rights culture becomes anchored within the Nigerian police department.

CHAPTER 24

Togo: Successfully Releasing Detainees

In the 1990s, the EU suspended development assistance to Togo because of serious human rights violations. Following bloodshed during an uprising in connection with presidential elections, international pressure was brought to bear and the situation gradually improved. In 2006, a political pact was reached with the opposition for the first time. In this context of a gradual buildup of democratic and human rights institutions, the international community was anxious to have an objective assessment of the human rights situation. The EU had even hinted at the possibility of lifting sanctions if my report were to show that the situation with regard to torture had improved significantly.

Such a set of circumstances is, clearly, ideal for a fact-finding mission since the government is eager to ensure that an independent evaluation takes place. Unlike many other missions, in this case I did not have to overcome obstacles. On the contrary, Prime Minister Yawovi Madji Agboyibo was so concerned about my well-being that he contacted me by telephone several times during our visits to places of detention to make sure that all was well.

On one occasion he called me just as intelligence officers were in the process of blocking my access to detainees they were responsible for. They were stunned when I passed my phone to them, suggesting they sort the matter out directly with the prime minister himself. There were no more problems after that fortuitous call.

On this mission, carried out in April 2007, along with BIM researchers Julia Kozma and Isabelle Tschan, I was joined by Hans-Petter Hougen, the Danish forensic expert, and Birgit Kainz-Labbe, an Austrian human rights expert who along with Safir Syed was henceforth responsible at OHCHR for my mandate and who brought to our team a good deal of experience from past duties with the OSCE in Central Asia.

Comparatively Better Conditions of Detention

Compared with 2005, the situation with regard to torture had improved significantly. Detainees were still being beaten by the police and gendarmerie to intimidate them and obtain confessions from them, but we did not see any signs of especially brutal torture such as in Nigeria or systematic torture as in Equatorial Guinea. Moreover, officials were quite open and often admitted without lengthy questioning that they occasionally did get carried away when faced with particularly rebellious detainees.

Detention conditions in prisons, barracks, police and gendarmerie stations were deplorable, as was the case in the majority of African states, but here too an attempt by the government was in evidence to shorten the police custody period and to improve conditions. As a result I appealed to the international community and in particular to the EU to support relevant measures to reform the justice system and to improve detention conditions as a part of their development assistance.

Unlike in a number of other states, Togo's code of criminal procedure contains relatively rigorous provisions regarding maximum periods of custody by the police or the gendarmerie. In principle, detainees suspected of a crime must be brought before a court within forty-eight hours. The public prosecutor's office or the court may extend this period by a further forty-eight hours if serious grounds exist. Although by contrast with states such as Nigeria, Equatorial Guinea, or Jamaica, we did not find any detainees who had been in police custody for months or even years, the interrogations did sometimes last two weeks before referral to a court or the prosecuting authorities. Given that the custody register was generally in fairly decent order, we decided to test this practice a little further, since it obviously encouraged the use of torture.

Freedom for the Chicken Thief

On 14 April 2007, we visited a small gendarmerie station in Sokode, in the interior of the country. The cells were extremely hot and stuffy, filthy, dark, malodorous, and infested with mosquitoes and insects. In these cells we found three frightened and completely naked men. The commanding officer assured us that he was simply following an instruction that all items of clothing had to be confiscated from detainees to protect them from possible suicide. I should add that this is a reason I have heard in Togo and elsewhere to justify the degrading practice of confiscating brassieres from women and even underwear from men.

Two detainees had already been in the cells for more than forty-eight hours and one of them claimed he had been lashed with a leather whip until he had confessed to stealing a chicken. The custody register indicated that the forty-eight-hour maximum period had been exceeded, which prompted us to ask the commanding officer why the young man had not been released. His reply was that the public prosecutor had extended the period. We responded with a request to see the corresponding paperwork. Impossible, came the reply, because it had been done over the telephone. Whereupon we asked to speak with the prosecutor by phone to verify this, but naturally the phone lines were down at that precise moment. Where could we meet with the prosecutor, we asked, but were informed that he was usually no longer at work at this time. Undeterred, I said we would very much like to visit him at his home.

It turned out that the home of the public prosecutor was not far at all from the gendarmerie station, so we, along with the gendarmerie commander, paid him a visit late that afternoon. He was astonished when we arrived at his home with our two UN off-road vehicles and a gendarmerie vehicle. I explained apologetically that we did not wish to disturb him for a long time, but that we simply wanted to know when he had extended the custody for a twenty-two-year-old chicken thief named Amayi Beindoune. At first he stared at me in disbelief. Then he stared at the gendarmerie commander, who was unable to utter a single word. Then he started to shout.

My first thought was that I was the target of his anger and that he was irate at being disturbed during his well-deserved afternoon rest (he was, after all, in his underwear) over such a trivial matter. Wrong. He was shouting at the gendarmerie commander. How dare he tell such bald-faced lies to these ladies and gentlemen from the United Nations? This was the first time he had even heard about this chicken thief and therefore had no idea that he was in custody. In fact, it had been a very long time since he had been contacted at all by the gendarmerie about a custody extension. Of course, such an extension could only be granted in writing. However, he would under no circumstances authorize a custody extension for the theft of a chicken.

In order to quell this outburst, genuine or feigned, I asked whether, in view of the fact that he had not granted a custody extension, I would be correct in assuming that the young man should be released immediately. Of course, he shouted, his ire still focused on the cowering commander. Would it be possible for us to have this instruction in writing? Certainly, he replied with a grin as he handed us a hastily scribbled piece of paper.

We hurried back to the gendarmerie station with this release order and told the young man he could pack up his things. The commander at this point declared that it would be preferable to release him in the morning, as it was late and it would take a good deal of time to prepare all of the papers required for his release. We were not willing to accept this, as we wanted to observe his release ourselves, and in the end the formalities lasted a mere half hour.

The young fellow was just as dumbfounded as the commander when we invited him to join us for a short drive in our vehicle until we were out of sight of the gendarmes. We thought the gendarmes might actually recapture him and beat him for exposing them in this shameful way, so we decided to give him some money for a taxi and our telephone numbers so that he could call us in case something untoward happened. As he walked away from us we saw for the first time what was written on the back of his T-shirt: "I hit a home run!" He called us that same evening as well as each of the following days to tell us happily that he had not been troubled by the gendarmerie anymore. He added that in his village, everyone now knew what an excellent institution the United Nations was.

We too were pleased with this unexpected success and applied this method to other police and gendarmerie stations. Thus, we cut short the custody of around twenty people and in fact, since word had spread in the meantime, we were able to obtain the release of detainees whose forty-eight-hour limit had lapsed, without having to find a prosecutor.

Follow-Up

In the context of the Atlas of Torture project carried out by the Ludwig Boltzmann Institute of Human Rights from 2012 to 2013, I was invited by the Togolese authorities with my team, which included Moritz Birk, Johanna Lober, and Tiphanie Crittin, to provide them with technical assistance in the implementation of my mission recommendations.

Unfortunately, I observed that overcrowding in filthy cells was still a worrisome issue despite a minister of human rights who was willing to improve the situation. In particular, we analyzed during our assessment mission that a very large number of detainees were still held in custody for months or even years without a trial and without being able to challenge their detention. Hence, we decided in partnership with the excellent NGO UCJG to help these "forgotten detainees" by reviving the very innovative system of "judicial clubs" created by UCJG that had been stopped due to a lack of funding. The idea was to train detainees to write habeas corpus petitions, complaints, and audience requests themselves. These detainees could then contact the authorities on behalf of their co-detainees, and actively seek a resolution of their cases. Two experienced prosecutors and a lawyer agreed to provide the necessary training to dozens of detainees in five prisons throughout the country. This empowering initiative meant that pretrial detainees no longer had to wait passively for justice to be served. The program's success was astonishing: in only one year, 586 detainees were released through this project. It clearly responded to a need that I had already identified in my visit to Sokode as special rapporteur. It also showed, however, that the criminal justice system had totally collapsed in Togo and that the authorities, despite their apparent willingness, had difficulties implementing my recommendations. For this reason, we decided, jointly with our partner UCJG, to also provide support to civil society organizations by helping with the establishment of a watchdog group called "Barometer Initiative," composed of four NGOs focused on torture prevention (UCJG, Amnesty International, CACIT, and ACAT). It aimed to measure the implementation of UN recommendations by the government and to raise the awareness of the population and the authorities regarding unfulfilled promises and weak commitments. This initiative still exists today and helped to strengthen the relationship among these key NGOs.

Aware that there was a dire need to shed light on detention conditions and give a voice to the powerless Togolese detainees, we also provided numerous training initiatives on detention monitoring to UCJG and the National Commission of Human Rights (NCHR). The Commission was in the process of establishing a National Preventive Mechanism (NPM) that was in charge of regularly visiting places of detention. We therefore also advised it in defining the model of NPM that would suit it best. Unfortunately, this process took longer than expected, and the NPM law was only passed at the National Assembly in March 2016. But at least there is now hope that this monitoring body will raise awareness on the fate of thousands of detainees.

CHAPTER 25

Sri Lanka: Perfect PR Strategy

I had already visited Sri Lanka in October 1999 on an official UN mission as a member of the Working Group on Enforced Disappearances. The mission was successful to the extent that, through tough negotiations, we were able to convince the government and families of disappeared persons to accept a settlement that provided families with financial support and social benefits in exchange for their acceptance of a legal death certificate. This enabled us to elucidate the fate of more than four thousand disappeared persons.

Striving for a Good Image

I was nevertheless not very optimistic when I approached the government again in 2006 in order to obtain an invitation for a torture fact-finding mission. The armed conflict with the Liberation Tigers of Tamil Eelam (LTTE) had taken a turn for the worse and the Norwegian-brokered cease-fire of 2002 was in tatters. The government and the army had decided that the conflict with the LTTE was not going to be resolved through negotiations but would require a military victory, which in the end is what happened.

At the time the government was very keen to have a positive public image and reacted very harshly to any form of criticism from outside, in particular from the United Nations. The way that Louise Arbour, UN high commissioner for human rights, or Sir John Holmes, under-secretary general for humanitarian affairs, were taken to task by members of the government for their entirely accurate criticism was completely outside the bounds of diplomatic courtesy. On the other hand, Sri Lanka was very eager to play a major part in the newly established Human Rights Council. It was a veritable masterstroke in diplomacy that a representative of a state under heavy criticism for grave and systematic human rights violations was elected to the post of vice president of the Human Rights Council. Thus, Sri Lanka had to undertake to cooperate closely with the experts of the Council, although the credibility of this institution was undermined in the process. This was probably one of the reasons I was able to carry out a mission to Sri Lanka in October 2007 without having to resort to protracted negotiations.

In contrast with the way other UN representatives were received, the government was very obliging toward me during my fact-finding mission and afterward. My seasoned team for this challenging mission included Safir Syed (Geneva), the BIM experts Julia Kozma and Isabelle Tschan, and the Scottish forensic medical expert Derrick Pounder.

Cancellation of the Mission Narrowly Averted

Although the security situation was unpredictable, we were able to move about fairly freely and unobserved and were able to visit the capital Colombo and surrounding area as well as the south (Galle), east (Trincomalee), and central (Kandy) parts of this island state. The LTTE leadership extended an invitation to visit them in an LTTE-controlled area in the north. At the time of my visit, the LTTE headquarters was in Kilinochi but the government, which had earlier given its permission, this one and only time did not allow the visit to take place. I had no alternative but to accept this decision, but it meant that we were unable to investigate torture accusations against the LTTE on the ground and I therefore had to withhold any assessment of the LTTE.

The government attempted to force me to accept a second condition after my arrival in Colombo, which I rejected out of hand. In view of the tense military situation and the constant danger of terrorist attacks, the government wanted to provide me with three bodyguards who would accompany me at all times and for the entire duration of my mission. That would have turned every single unannounced visit into an absurd situation. At the beginning I could not even move about the hotel freely without these persons following my every step. At one point they even tried to push their way into the United Nations vehicle, but our French UN security guard Jean-Louis Dominguez unceremoniously ejected them from the car.

We wasted almost two days negotiating with Mahinda Samarasinghe, minister of disaster management and human rights (this ministry's portfolio speaks volumes about the priority of human rights in Sri Lanka; we jokingly referred to him as "Minister of Human Rights Disaster Management"), until we finally managed to convince him that I would have to abort the mission if the government continued to monitor my every move. As he gave in, he cautioned that I would be solely responsible should something untoward happen to us.

In order to placate him, the United Nations assigned an additional extremely experienced security officer to our group, Godfrey Gunasekera, who was impressive above and beyond his towering physique. He had headed the Police Academy of Sri Lanka for many years, and even high-ranking police officers had immense respect for this distinguished man.

Praise Notwithstanding Strong Criticism

There was no doubt that torture was widespread in Sri Lanka. However, since it appeared to be implemented less frequently during routine criminal proceedings than I had originally expected based on NGO reports and other sources, in my report I could not describe it as systematic torture, as I did for example in the case of Nepal.

Because systematic torture is the strongest form of condemnation of a state and should in principle lead to its expulsion from the Human Rights Council and possibly to the establishment of a country-specific special rapporteur mandate, the fact that I did not report systematic torture was cunningly used by the government in its PR strategy. Although I reported that particularly brutal torture methods and a routine use of such interrogation techniques by the military and special units such as the Terrorist Investigation Department (TID) were in evidence when the government dealt with Tamils and especially those suspected of belonging to the LTTE, the government praised the objectivity of my report in the media and in the Human Rights Council. It stressed repeatedly that the special rapporteur on torture had found no evidence of systematic torture in spite of all of the false accusations against the state.

When I presented my report in Geneva, in addition to the "Human Rights Disaster Management Minister" Samarasinghe, three other ministers had flown to Geneva to see me and thank me for the professionalism of my report. The defense minister even invited me to train his officers in torture prevention techniques.

Documenting the Most Brutal Forms of Torture

Gradually we began to fear that the true situation in Sri Lanka was possibly much worse than we had realized during our mission and what I had documented in my report. I set out to read the report once again very carefully and noted that I had included explicit descriptions of the most vicious imaginable torture methods: burns all over the body made with soldering irons and a heated piece of metal, suspension in a variety of positions ("strappado," "butchery," "reversed butchery," "parrot's perch") and by the thumbs, which were bound together by a piece of wire (Derrick Pounder noted that he had never seen this extraordinarily painful method used in any other country). I had also noted many different types of beatings, including on the soles of the feet ("falanga"), squeezing and beating testicles, and other forms of sexual torture. Attempts by authorities, e.g., the TID, to hide detainees from us were just as comprehensively documented as reprisals against detainees who had the courage to speak with us.

I would venture to say that I do not believe the report is too uncritical when read in its entirety. On the contrary, there are practically no other countries for which I documented in great detail so many cases of savage torture. But the government's PR strategy, like a mantra repeating that I had uncovered no systematic torture, performed simultaneously with demonstrations of their excellent cooperation with me, was a hit with the audience: Sri Lanka was not expelled from the Human Rights Council. In addition, NGOs and individual states were unsuccessful in their attempts to appoint a country-specific special rapporteur to investigate the grave and systematic human rights violations in the country, even after the military annihilation of the LTTE and subsequent terrifying persecution of Tamils.

In May 2009, when the EU was finally able to push through a special session of the UN Human Rights Council on Sri Lanka, the government managed to turn even that situation to its own advantage. Sri Lanka's successful lobbying led to a majority of the states in the Council finding that in fact the grave human rights violations had not been committed by the military or the police but by the rebellious Tamils!

CHAPTER 26

Indonesia: Three "Smoking Guns"

In our internal fact-finding jargon we use the term "smoking gun" for situations in which we are able to directly observe torture almost as it is happening, as if we are peeking over the shoulder of a torturer hard at work. This is never actually supposed to happen. The timing of any of my fact-finding missions is worked out in advance with governments. I have to assume that the government informs all relevant services and departments (police, military, intelligence, justice, prisons, psychiatric facilities, etc.) about the timing of my mission and the agreed investigation terms. I would also assume that those responsible would instruct their employees to cooperate with us and to avoid creating any cause for complaint by, for example, refraining from torture at least during my mission. As my missions have shown, this clearly does not mean that all traces of torture can be readily wiped out. But finding that the weapon used for the crime might still be "smoking" was something I had not expected.

Again, on this mission to Indonesia in November 2007, I had a thoroughly experienced team with me: Birgit Kainz-Labbé (Geneva), Isabelle Tschan, and Roland Schmidt (BIM), as well as our forensic medical expert from Portugal, Duarte Vieira. We found a total of three "smoking guns." As a rule, such situations lead to intractable problems and moral dilemmas.

A Police Station in Jakarta

In a sizable police station in east Jakarta, we came upon seventy-three detainees, most of whom reported they had been beaten when they were interrogated. Some had clearly visible and very recent traces of physical abuse which

Duarte Vieira documented in detail. The interrogations usually did not take place in the cell blocks but in specially equipped interrogation rooms or directly in the offices of the criminal police, which detainees described or sketched for us, mostly fairly accurately. The reason we asked them to do this was to verify detainees' statements and to help us find torture instruments, which are not too difficult to locate.

When we opened the door to one of the interrogation rooms in the narcotics department, we chanced upon an ongoing interrogation of a suspected drug dealer. His face was quite swollen, one eye was bloodshot, and we later found clear indications on his person that he had been beaten in various places. When we asked the criminal police officer to leave the room, the torture victim suddenly realized the explosive nature of the situation and tried to explain to us that he was not a detainee at all but a close acquaintance of the officer and had merely stopped in for a visit. His fear had evidently made him overlook the facts that not only was his face swollen but he was handcuffed to his chair. After the situation had been sorted out and the officer had left the room, we interviewed and examined the detainee. His statement about the beatings sustained was corroborated by the medical examination.

Now what? The detainee was quite fearful, very likely not without cause, that as soon as we left the building he would be beaten once again. It would have made little sense to warn the head of the criminal police about reprisals since the interview had revealed that he was directly involved in the torture. When I urged the officers to release him, they refused because of his alleged role in drug trafficking. Our only options were to speak with the chief of police, who naturally assured us there would be no reprisals, and then hope that he would keep his promise.

Yogyakarta Police Headquarters

We received a nearly hostile reception from the officers on duty at the Yogyakarta police headquarters, and it took a good deal of time for us to gain access to the cells. The tactic here consisted of increasingly higher-ranking police officers diverting us from the cell block, evidently to prepare the detainees for our interviews with them and to threaten them with reprisals should they dare show us their injuries.

The eight cells were arranged around the perimeter of a square-shaped inner courtyard which could be observed from outside by the officers. We noticed immediately that many of the forty-eight detainees had fresh wounds. They were very afraid to speak with us because the officers looked in frequently to see who we were speaking with. My repeated requests to the police commander to ensure that our interviews could not be heard or observed by his officers served only to exacerbate an already aggressive atmosphere. I asked two members of my team to remain outside the cells to prevent the officers from peering into the courtyard during our interviews, but this did not stop them and they even tried repeatedly to enter the courtyard.

All we could do was to speak to each of the detainees for the same length of time so that no conclusions could be drawn about the significance of the interviews or about alleged complaints of torture. Duarte Vieira tried hard to have all of the detainees remove their shirts, but precisely those whose bodies bore clear evidence of recent ill-treatment were terrified of being examined. Some of the marks indicated that the torture had been quite severe. In some cases we even found injuries to the legs that we were familiar with from Nigeria, caused by a gunshot from a short distance.

The detainees were able to describe very accurately the offices where they had been tortured. The officials tried to impede our access to the offices of the criminal police by stressing that my United Nations mandate only allowed the inspection of detainees and places of detention but did not extend to the offices of the officials. They would not accept the fact that detainees continued to be deprived of their liberty during interrogations. Yet again I had to muster my full authority as special rapporteur in order to finally gain access to the offices and interrogation rooms, but the officials followed us every step of the way.

Suddenly we came upon a young man in the drug trafficking department who, immediately before we entered the room, had been severely beaten with an iron bar and a plastic hose by four police officers (whose identities we checked). His girlfriend, who had been arrested with him and had had to listen to his screaming from the adjoining room, testified that he had been tortured. She was beside herself with fear and as she spoke with us she had numerous crying fits. As we prepared to enter the torture room, once again a loud argument erupted with the head of the drug trafficking department.

We found the torture instruments in the interrogation room and they were exactly as the young man had described them. The plastic hose in particular had a unique shape. Duarte Vieira had been at a loss to explain certain wounds during his medical examination of the young man, but could now see that the shape of the white plastic hose was completely consistent with the marks left by the beatings on the young man's upper body.

At this point the four torturers no longer attempted to deny anything. The situation was all too clear and no further evidence was needed. But we now had to deal with both the officials who were furious at having been disturbed in the middle of what appeared to be their routine torture session and the young couple who were pleading with us to protect them. But how?

Our insisting that they should be released was in vain. Isabelle Tschan even offered to spend a night with the couple in police custody to protect them from reprisals. But time was not on our side as we had to return to Jakarta. Once again, all I could do was to forcefully remind the chief of police that reprisals of any kind against the detainees that should come to our attention might well lead to his immediate removal. He gave me his word in front of the couple. Both the young couple and we knew that this promise was not worth much in light of the atmosphere of fear and violence in this police station. The frightened look in their eyes as we departed was hard for me to bear.

The entire team felt dejected as we made our way, very late, to the airport to catch our flight to Jakarta. On the flight, we had a lengthy fundamental debate about the opportunities and limitations of my mandate. What was the value added of putting these two young people at risk again for the sake of documenting as accurately as possible yet another unambiguous example of torture?

The Wamena Police Headquarters

In addition to densely populated Java we visited the islands of Sulawesi and Bali as well as West Papua (Irian Jaya), where we also flew to the impenetrable highlands which are not yet accessible by road. The indigenous people who live in this area have been spared most of the "blessings" of Western civilization and are locked in a political and to some extent armed struggle against colonization by Indonesia. Their legal system, not unlike that of nearby Papua New Guinea, is strongly characterized by notions of traditional and customary law. Adjacent to each sizable police station there is a special "round table," surrounded by a pond, where conflicts between families or ethnic groups are supposed to be settled with mediation by the police. There is no clear dividing line between civil and criminal law, such that even relatively serious crimes (robbery, rape, bodily harm, or even murder) can be settled through appropriate payment if the victim's family agrees. Pigs are considered to be a valuable form of payment.

When we walked into the police headquarters in Wamena in the highlands of West Papua, Roland Schmidt witnessed this form of police mediation in a room next to the entrance. A young, strongly built man named Beremius Wanimbo had been accused by a family from a remote village of having raped a thirteen-year-old girl belonging to that family. The family elder had then forcibly taken him to the police headquarters in Wamena. The family and the police proposed that this conflict might be settled with a payment of US$50 to the victim's family. But because the young man vigorously denied having committed this act, he was obliged to remove his shirt and three police officers, under the supervision of their supervisor Erwin B., began to beat and kick him. Just before we entered the police station, the head of the other family had punched him in the face hard enough to make him bleed from his nose and mouth. The alleged rape victim stood frightened in a corner of the room. What had transpired was so obvious that no one tried to deny anything.

First we interviewed Beremius Wanimbo, who was trembling like a leaf and crying uncontrollably. Duarte Vieira's medical examination concluded that his injuries were the result of blows he had just sustained. As the chief of police was not present, we went with Erwin B. and the three other officers who had beaten him to see the chief of the criminal police to report what had happened and to ask him what he intended to do about it. He replied that it would be best to wait for the chief of police, who had already been contacted and was on his way.

The chief arrived shortly, and he listened closely to my report, which was confirmed by the four officers. Presently he stood up and embarked upon a lengthy speech. He said that I must have been sent by God himself. In all of the years that he had been in charge, it had never happened that one of his officers had abused anyone. Now, on the very day, the only day when something as outrageous as this took place, I should show up with my team. He went on to describe himself as a devout, God-fearing man who detested any form of violence. He was thankful to our Lord from the bottom of his heart that he had sent me to Wamena on this memorable day. In order to gently put a stop to further delving into religious considerations, I asked him what measures he intended to take. He reiterated that nothing of the sort had ever occurred before but that he was going to begin an internal investigation immediately and that the necessary disciplinary measures would be taken.

I thanked him and we drove to a hospital in the vicinity with Beremius Wanimbo, the thirteen-year-old girl, and two police officers to have them both examined and treated. The female medical doctor on duty explained to me that the police came to the hospital regularly with injured detainees to have the injuries documented, but that these medical reports were only given to the police and never to the detainees. I was able to obtain a copy of this report, but only as a result of persistence and persuasion. The doctor seemed to be intimidated by the two officers and somewhat overwhelmed by the situation in general. No injuries were found on the girl, but the doctor was not able to exclude that she had been raped. Under no circumstances did she wish to keep Beremius Wanimbo, who was still distraught, in the hospital, so she gave him some basic medical attention and was happy to turn him back over to the police. She was not willing to answer my question about whether she had determined ill-treatment by the police in other cases. Although we could not know whether Beremius Wanimbo actually had raped the girl, I nevertheless did not want to let him spend the night with the police and decided to ask the chief of police to release him. He agreed immediately, as no requests from me could be turned down since I had come to him as an emissary of the Lord himself. The disciplinary investigation was in full swing as we finally left the police station toward evening with Beremius Wanimbo. He was puzzled about what was happening to him and I was not entirely comfortable about having intervened so forcefully in the course of the traditional criminal justice system and for potentially shielding a rapist from his "fair" punishment. The girl, who had said nothing at all and would not talk to us, seemed glad when he was gone.

The next morning we returned unannounced to the police station. The four officers had indeed been admonished and sentenced to twenty-one days of disciplinary detention. Erwin B., as the ranking officer, had also been deprived of all privileges for one year. The criminal investigations of torture were still under way, the chief of police proudly informed us. We also visited Erwin B. in his cell. He seemed somewhat dejected but assured us that no violence had been used against him. He was having trouble understanding what it was about this relatively mild case of use of force to "determine the truth," compared with other situations, that had led to such a disproportionate effort and reaction. We told him we believed that it was probably connected with our presence, which did not necessarily endear us to him. At any rate, this disciplinary measure was greatly exaggerated, he told us when we departed, seemingly not too upset with us anymore. He said it was nice that we had been concerned about his well-being.

CHAPTER 27

Denmark and Greenland: The Principle of Normalization

Denmark (including Greenland) is the only one out of eighteen countries investigated for which we received no complaint of torture, neither before nor during our mission in May 2008, and about which we found no indications whatsoever of torture. Even the three minor accusations of ill-treatment of detainees were not quite credible but were nonetheless taken very seriously by the government and immediately investigated. The Danish example demonstrates that it is entirely possible to eradicate torture, if the necessary political will is present and a commensurate human rights culture is promoted among the police and in the prison system. For this mission, my team was composed of Isabelle Tschan, Safir Syed, and the forensic medical expert Jonathan Beynon, who, for a change, had little to do on this particular mission.

Prevention and Social Reintegration Instead of Retribution

The high human rights standards in prisons and other places of detention, including pre-deportation detention, were as impressive as the absence of torture. The Danish prison system has been guided for many years by the "principle of normalization," according to which life behind bars is as similar as possible to life in the normal outside world. Whereas in many countries of the world detainees are treated "worse than animals" (as they themselves describe it) and are deprived of practically all of their human rights, including the right to live in dignity, in Denmark detainees are viewed as "clients."

Deprivation of liberty is considered to be sufficiently severe that the administration of prisons considers it its duty to make life in detention as comfortable as possible for the "clients." This was exactly the opposite in most of the countries I visited. This approach was not only in the interest of the clients but also of prison management because satisfied detainees were less likely to cause trouble, escape, begin hunger strikes, do harm to themselves, and were less violent toward fellow inmates or prison staff. It is hard to imagine a better way to illustrate the contrast between a criminal justice system based on retribution and a modern criminal justice system that incorporates principles of prevention and social rehabilitation of offenders.

Open Prisons

The "principle of normalization" means first of all that prisons are run as open establishments to the maximum extent possible. In Greenland there are no completely closed prisons; detainees leave the prisons in the morning just as ordinary people leave their homes to go to work, train or educate themselves, or engage in other "normal" activities. In the evening they return to their accommodation in prison. They are actually locked up only in special circumstances, such as in the case of prisoners awaiting trial due to danger of collusion (who are fairly often kept for long periods in solitary confinement) or detainees who have received a disciplinary punishment. Sex offenders who have committed serious offenses and are often recidivists are transferred to a special institution in Denmark because there are no appropriate facilities for them in the open prison system of Greenland. Even Denmark itself has few completely closed prisons. Leave taken during detention to visit families or friends fosters the subsequent social rehabilitation of detainees and reduces recidivism rates.

Closed Prisons

Closed prisons are also as open as possible on the inside. Detainees are practically never locked up in cells. Generally, they sleep in single bedrooms, sometimes even in small apartments equipped with kitchens and bathrooms. But the doors are never locked. During the day detainees can move about freely in the prison or at least in certain zones and can occupy themselves with work, further education, sports, or other activities so that they do not have to merely kill time, as is the case in most prisons around the world. Self-determination is one of the main goals of normality. To be able to decide for oneself how one wishes to spend time in prisons, instead of being rigidly subjected to prison regulations and discipline, makes a huge difference for the self-esteem of detainees. The same applies to the right to privacy, which in China and many other countries is non-existent for those behind bars. An important element of normality is also the ability to withdraw occasionally to one's own little corner or better yet to a private room, to avoid being constantly exposed to the peer pressure of other prisoners and the watchful eye of prison guards.

Visits from Relatives

Another important element of normalization is regular visits from family members and friends in a relaxed and, to the extent possible, normal environment. In many of the prisons I visited, the strict limitations surrounding visits were the reason for most of the complaints from detainees. In the post-Communist states, for example, visiting hours are severely limited for detainees with long sentences, although they are in desperate need of visits as their only contact with the outside world. When spouses or children are able to visit, they are often allowed only a few minutes and are separated from detainees by a window or bars, which precludes badly needed physical contact. It is shocking for children to see their father or mother in prison uniforms, possibly in handcuffs, through a window without even being able to touch or embrace them. Restrictions such as these, which amount to another form of punishment or disciplinary measure, are deemed necessary for security reasons.

Denmark is an excellent example of how alternatives to traditional forms of punishment and detention can and do work. In the Vridsloselille prison we were impressed by the rooms set aside for children to visit their parents. These rooms were equipped with stuffed animals, colorful and attractive pictures, games, puzzles, and toys, such that children could forget that they were in a prison. When Daddy wears normal clothes, there are no guards around, and he can communicate freely with his children, play with them and hug them, then the result is a normal visit, much like when other children visit their parents at work. The detainees are allowed to retain their dignity and the children are not traumatized. The cost is very low but the effects are far-reaching.

No Gender Segregation

A most unusual feature of the prison system in Denmark and Greenland is that it does not require gender segregation. In principle, detainees of different genders may live together in a room or small apartment, even if they are not married, as long as such an arrangement is based on mutual consent. Naturally, this degree of sexual freedom, which I have not seen in any other country, can lead to problems such as rape or dependence of women on dominating male detainees. Since women make up only a relatively small percentage of detainees, as in all parts of the world, in Denmark they are obviously in great demand. The strongest and most dominating male detainees are in the best position to protect "their" women from being harassed. The marriage rate in Danish prisons is significantly higher than in the general population.

We discussed these issues with female detainees, including some who had been raped in prison and had borne children who had had to be given up after three years. They were unanimous in their view that the Danish "normality" system, in spite of its undeniable drawbacks and risks, was preferable to segregated prisons.

Prison directors and politicians have also explicitly defended this system, notwithstanding the fact that it is inconsistent with international standards. However, a careful assessment of the pros and cons indicates that the advantages far outweigh the drawbacks. A segregation of the genders is in fact not "normal" and because one cannot give up sexual desire at the prison gate along with personal effects, it leads to great pressure on young detainees to engage in homosexual relations although they are heterosexual in their normal lives. Those who do not freely give in to this pressure are often raped and otherwise brutalized, which leads among other things to an elevated HIV rate among the prison population. Generally speaking, exclusively male prisons are much more violent than women's prisons or mixed places of detention. It should also be pointed out that mixed-gender prisons, precisely because they are more "normal," are a better starting point for rehabilitation after detention.

Is the Principle Exportable?

The Danish "normalization principle," including gender mixing, cannot simply be transferred to other countries in spite of its obvious advantages. This is because a large degree of freedom can of course also be abused, especially when one is not accustomed to such latitude. I believe that this principle can only work in countries that have an advanced human rights culture generally. If the "normality" of a society is characterized by mutual respect and observance of human rights, then this normality can also work in prisons. The most important prerequisite is a human rights education, which should begin as early as kindergarten.

CHAPTER 28

Moldova: Torture in the Form of Trafficking in Women

In July 2008, I undertook a joint mission with Yakin Erturk, the then UN special rapporteur on violence against women, to Moldova, including the autonomous region of Transnistria, which declared independence from Moldova in 1990 but is not recognized as an independent state. My support team on this mission included the very experienced Birgit Kainz-Labbé (Geneva), Julia Kozma, and Isabelle Tschan (BIM), as well as Duarte Vieira, our forensic medical expert from Portugal.

As is the case in other post-Soviet states, torture and ill-treatment are still widespread during the initial period spent in police custody, and the conditions of detention for the most part are inhumane. On the other hand, the government appeared to be genuinely aiming to improve the situation and aligning itself with European standards. I therefore made a follow-up visit in September 2009 during which we trained members of a recently created national commission (responsible for undertaking preventive visits to places of detention) in methods of investigating and documenting torture. In addition, I continued to advise the government of Moldova, assisted by my team at the Ludwig Boltzmann Institute of Human Rights (Julia Kozma and Johanna Lober) under a major EU project involving measures to combat torture and improve detention conditions. At the end of November 2011, a two-day conference was held in Chisinau at which a concrete action plan was created to implement my recommendations with the government and civil society.

Aside from cases where torture had been used to obtain confessions, we were particularly disturbed during our visit by the following three situations: conditions in psychiatric institutions, the treatment of detainees who had been sentenced to life imprisonment or (in Transnistria) to death, and the fate of trafficked women.

Appalling Conditions in Psychiatric Wards

The psychiatric hospital in Balti, with more than seven hundred male and female patients, is starkly reminiscent of the Soviet era. We visited the children's ward, where we immediately noticed that even very young children had been subdued with sedatives. The closed section of the hospital was particularly dreadful. Many people, young and old, men and women, were lying in their beds in a cramped room, completely apathetic and sadly reminiscent of living corpses. They were completely unresponsive and spent the entire day in their beds. The armed guards stationed at the entrances to this room could have been dispensed with since sedatives had evidently robbed these people of any desire to escape.

Cruel Conditions of Detention

Moldova, along with other post-Soviet states, still follows the retributive criminal justice philosophy according to which detention conditions are especially severe for individuals who have received long sentences, life sentences, or the death penalty (which is officially still on the books in Transnistria as well as Abkhazia and South Ossetia, breakaway provinces of Georgia). The drastic limitations of visiting hours, the incommunicado detention, and extreme security measures are imposed not as security or disciplinary measures, because detainees are known to be especially dangerous in detention or have committed additional crimes, but because they are part and parcel of the penalty handed down by the court. Yet, there is at least a partial acknowledgment in these states that prisons are not necessarily only places of punishment but that they should offer detainees some measure of rehabilitation and that particularly good behavior during detention should lead to an easing of detention conditions and early release.

In a prison in Hlinaia in Transnistria I spoke with a tall, slim, and agile forty-two-year-old man who had been given the death penalty in July 2003 for what was evidently a political crime. He had been in strict solitary confinement for the last five years. He spent twenty-three hours a day in his cell and was permitted access to a small courtyard to exercise one hour a day without ever seeing any other detainees. Once every four months he was allowed a visit of not more than four hours, but he refused to allow his three children to see him in this condition. His cell had three separate locks and each of the three keys was carried by a different guard. If someone entered his cell, the detainee's hands were handcuffed behind his back. He appeared to be so used to the cuffs that he was able to stretch his arms over his head with the handcuffs on his wrists and could even light a cigarette without our help. The walls of his prison cell were covered with colorful wallpaper depicting a jungle scene and a huge waterfall.

The long period of isolation, which I qualify as torture, had clearly scarred his mental health. He was unable to discuss anything but the unfairness of his conviction, about which he intended to lodge a complaint with the European Court of Human Rights in Strasbourg because in a similar case (*Iliascu*) the Court had ruled that there had been a violation of the European Human Rights Convention by both Moldova and the Russian Federation.

Trafficking in Women

As the poorest country in Europe, Moldova is particularly attractive for traffickers in women. Thousands of Moldovan women are sold in the wealthier European countries by well-organized criminal gangs, where they are held as slaves, abused, and forced into prostitution or domestic work. Those who manage to escape and go to the police are often treated not as victims requiring immediate assistance but as illegal migrants and deported back to their countries of origin as swiftly as possible, where they often wind up back in the hands of their tormentors and the cycle of torture starts all over again.

In spite of the fact that both the United Nations and the Council of Europe have banned such practices and have recognized trafficked human beings as victims of modern slavery and therefore as victims of human rights violations (the former in the so-called Palermo Protocol, as it is known, to the International Convention on Organized Crime of 2000, and the latter with a specific instrument known as the Convention on Action against Trafficking in Human Beings of 2005), little has changed as a result of the spreading xenophobia and extremely restrictive immigration laws in Europe.

I would like to depict this situation, which I qualify as torture or inhuman treatment as a result of a state's failure to protect, by using the example of twenty-two-year-old Annushka, whom we met and interviewed in a women's shelter run by a private organization in Chisinau. In November 2006 a stranger approached her in a park in Chisinau and promised that he could arrange a well-paid job for her in a retirement home in a rich country in Europe. As a diabetic who could hardly afford insulin, she agreed to the arrangement along with another woman and was promptly shipped off to Switzerland via a circuitous route through Poland and Italy. In Geneva she was locked in a room in a house where nobody could hear her screams. She was given little food and no insulin and as a result, her eyesight swiftly deteriorated. At the time of our interview with her, she was already completely blind.

Because she refused to work as a prostitute in a brothel, she was routinely beaten by the man who had approached her in Chisinau. One day, as he was entering her room, she managed to escape by hitting him on the head with a chair and running away. She was unable to remember what had happened afterward. When she regained consciousness, she was lying on a park bench with a broken leg. A woman took her to a clinic where she was hospitalized for three months.

Despite the fact that she had at the time already lost half of her eyesight, she was "ausgeschafft," which is Swiss bureaucratic German for "deported," to Moldova in February 2007. With assistance from the Red Cross, she was picked up at the airport by a representative of the women's shelter and taken there along with her eighteen-year-old sister. Since November 2007 she has been completely blind but her sister assists her. She has no money and no idea what she can do next. She does not dare leave her hiding place because she's afraid that the man who took her to Switzerland and locked her up there might find her again.

This case is one of many thousands taking place in the twenty-first century in Europe and in many other parts of the world. Trafficking in women has become one of the three most lucrative businesses of organized crime, and for reasons associated with hostility toward foreigners, governments do no more than take half-hearted measures to contain this modern form of torture and slavery.

Follow-Up

The advice we provided to the Moldovan authorities in the framework of the EU-funded Atlas of Torture project, which was designed as a follow-up to my recommendations made as UN special rapporteur on torture, focused on two cross-cutting issues to address the situation of torture and ill-treatment described above: strengthening the fight against impunity, and reinforcing the system of preventive visits to places of detention.

To strengthen the fight against widespread impunity for torture and ill-treatment, I had recommended revising the respective provisions in the criminal code and criminal procedure code. With our technical advice and the promotion of broad civil society participation in a legal amendment process, we supported Moldova in changing the legal classification of torture from a "less severe crime" with very lenient sentences (of two to five years' imprisonment) to a "serious crime" with sentences as long as fifteen years depending on the gravity of the circumstances. If implemented by the judicial authorities, this provision can become a real deterrent to the use of torture to obtain confessions or for any other purpose.

As a country routinely condemned by the European Court of Human Rights for ineffective investigations into allegations of torture and facing loud international criticism for the weakness and inaction of the judicial authorities in combating impunity, Moldova had established specialized anti-torture prosecutors. Our project supported these prosecutors in developing a detailed internal manual on how to investigate and prosecute cases of torture and ill-treatment in line with the newly amended legislative framework. At the same time, we promoted the capacity of defense lawyers in taking individual complaints to court in order to strengthen the "demand side" of the justice system.

With regard to the deplorable state of the conditions of detention in Moldovan prisons and psychiatric institutions, we continued our work with the national Ombuds-Office and the Ministry of Justice to reinforce the system for undertaking effective preventive visits to places of detention. In particular, we combined our efforts with the Office of the UN and national civil society to advise the Moldovan government in the revision of the widely criticized national mechanism for the prevention of torture.

CHAPTER 29

Equatorial Guinea: Systematic Torture as Government Policy

Equatorial Guinea is one of the worst dictatorships in the world. Although the situation in this former Spanish colony, situated between Cameroon and Gabon, has improved somewhat since the overthrow of long-term dictator Macias Nguema, his successor Teodoro Obiang nowadays completely measures up to him as far as implementation of repression and brutality is concerned. However, owing to the discovery of significant oil reserves, which are exploited mainly by American companies, this dictator can count on the support of the United States, and has been, at least during the Bush administration, more or less regarded as respectable.

A desire for recognition on the part of the international community was most likely the reason for inviting me there. In March 2004 a failed coup attempt had taken place by a group of South African mercenaries under the leadership of Englishman Simon Mann, and with the support of well-known financiers like Mark Thatcher, son of the former British prime minister. My mission was originally planned for February 2008, but was postponed by the government at the last minute. The reason, seemingly, was that exactly at this point in time Simon Mann was being handed over from Zimbabwe to Equatorial Guinea.

Government-Mandated Torture

Although I had supposed that my mission here, like my mission to Russia, would be postponed indefinitely, the government kept its word, and we were able to enter the country in November 2008. My team consisted of Birgit Kainz-Labbé (Geneva) and Isabelle Tschan, as well as Johanna Lober, who was new to the BIM team and who immediately experienced her "baptism of fire" with this difficult mission. Derrick Pounder would have his hands full as our medical forensic expert. And Roger Kaminker would prove his unique qualities as an interpreter and in other capacities, qualities that would be in especially high demand in the course of such a challenging mission. Last, the professionalism of our UN security officer Antonio Moreira would be sorely put to the test by a number of unpleasant incidents.

Perhaps the government had supposed that it could control us so well that we would find only minor evidence of torture. Although in the end access to military installations was forbidden to us, we had relatively unhindered access to police stations and prisons, both on the island of Bioko where the capital Malabo is situated and on the African mainland (Rio Muni). Our investigations, which were confirmed by Derrick Pounder, revealed that both political and criminal prisoners in police custody, especially in Malabo and in Bata, the largest city on the mainland, were systematically tortured, and that this happened with direct support from, and due to direct orders from, the government and the president.

The methods of torture encompassed a wide repertoire. They ranged from blows to the entire body including the soles of the feet, and electric shocks, and hanging in the so-called "Ethiopian position" between two tables, to burning with candles and inhalation of the candle smoke. After lengthy negotiations in the two largest police stations we gained access to the torture chambers, and we were even able to photograph the instruments of torture that prisoners had described to us, such as a car battery with starter cables that were placed on especially sensitive points of the body.

As the government began to realize that we were experiencing some success in gathering evidence, massive pressure was exerted on the head of the UN diplomatic mission in Equatorial Guinea, aimed at bringing us back from the mainland to the capital. However, Kiari Liman, a tough, experienced, and admirable diplomat from Chad, remained steadfast, and explained to the government, in so many words, that he had no influence over independent experts working for the UN.

A Courageous Opposition Politician

At the closing conference we sat across from the top military, police, and prison officials, plus five members of the government, a situation that was more than a little intimidating. Next to Foreign Minister Pastor Micha Ondo Bile were the minister of the interior, the minister of justice, the minister for national security, and the deputy defense minister, who all did me the honor of attending. Without any hint of emotion they listened to my report about systematic torture and wretched conditions in police custody: dark and filthy cells, where prisoners were kept without food for long periods; a lack of toilet facilities so severe that prisoners urinated in water bottles brought to them by family members, and performed their necessary bodily functions in plastic bags in which their families had brought them food. Then the feared Security Minister General Manuel Nguema Mba retorted that this was all propaganda and that I had no evidence.

However, he prudently refused my offer to accompany me to police headquarters, only ten minutes away, in order to witness my claims firsthand. Interior Minister Clemente Engonga Nguema Onguene thereupon got up and declared that he had proof that there was no truth to my claims. What proof, I asked. The thing was, they had had me watched, at every step, by the secret service. I countered that, of course, I had known that all along, and was still waiting for his proof. Triumphantly he announced that I had been speaking with members of the opposition.

Here it should be noted that all opposition parties are forbidden in Equatorial Guinea, with one sole exception. This one legal opposition party had exactly one representative among the one hundred members of parliament. This representative, who apparently served as a fig leaf for the regime's democratic façade, was an exceedingly courageous man, who had even founded a human rights organization and continually denounced various human rights violations. There was no other independent organization that dealt with the human rights situation in the country. NGOs were forbidden and nonexistent. Even the International Committee of the Red Cross had left the country.

So we had decided to meet in Bata with the parliamentary opposition member who dealt with human rights. That was no easy undertaking. The driver of my UN vehicle was an experienced and fearless older man whose perseverance I admired, as he again and again exuded personal authority and asserted himself, with his calm and decisive demeanor, against soldiers at military control points who refused to let us through. However, when I told him of my intention to visit the human rights representative of the opposition, to speak with witnesses and victims of human rights violations, he explained to me that I simply could not ask that of him, even though he was himself under the protection of the UN. His family would have to reckon with severe reprisals, and his wife would lose her job. Even the taxi driver to whom we paid a good deal of money to make this trip only dared to drive us to the outskirts of our destination, and we had to arrange for two more rides before we finally reached our destination in the evening. The stories of torture victim interviewees that we listened to that evening, by candlelight in a remote hut, were some of the worst I ever heard. However, I could include none of that in my report, because these people made me swear to secrecy in the strongest degree.

To return to the minister of the interior: The very fact that, in addition to meeting with representatives of the government, I had also dared to meet with a representative of the parliamentary opposition, was for him enough proof that I could not submit an objective report! There was no point in contradicting him. To defend the local coworkers of the United Nations team in this country from further reprisals, and to be able to leave the country intact and healthy, I abruptly cancelled the planned press conference in Malabo, and left for Geneva.

The Black Beach Prison

"Black Beach" is the name of one of the most feared prisons in Africa. It is situated on the sea at the edge of Malabo. However, in order to reach this prison one must fight one's way through a huge military complex with many checkpoints. We had to leave all of our equipment behind upon entry, even though I had received explicit permission from the government to bring along cameras and video cameras.

This prison had lost some of its aspect of horror, at least on the surface, due to a general renovation that had taken place shortly before our visit. Political prisoners, including the mercenaries who had been sentenced for the attempted coup, were kept away from the other prisoners in a strictly segregated high-security sector. They were all kept in solitary confinement in single cells. Nick du Toit was, like the majority of the other South Africans, arrested in March 2004 during the coup attempt, and given a sentence of many years' duration. He said that his confession was given under torture. During the first six weeks of his imprisonment he was kept in an exceptionally small cell in the old prison, with his hands bound behind his back. During the following four months his hands and feet were chained together in such a way that he could not move. Then the chains were removed from his feet but he had to wear handcuffs for an additional year. Later, instead of the handcuffs he was once again obliged to wear chains on his feet. At the time of our visit he had already spent more than four years in full solitary confinement, and his health had suffered immeasurably.

The other South Africans had not fared any better. Only Simon Mann, who was handed over from Zimbabwe in February 2008, was in a better mood. He had obviously fully cooperated with Security Minister General Nguema Mba from the very beginning, and therefore obtained privileged treatment despite his solitary confinement. Every day he received food specially prepared for him at the Hotel Paraiso in Malabo. One day the minister even brought an exercise machine to his cell as a gift. In comparison to the prison conditions in Zimbabwe, which he described as indescribably horrid and inhuman, the Black Beach prison was virtually a paradise. He also had firm hope that he might be released in the foreseeable future. He was, in fact, released in November 2009 and returned to Great Britain, where he wrote his memoirs, while his colleagues continued to languish in Black Beach.

An Investigation Without Consequences

In spite of our evidence of systematic torture and my extremely critical report, the United Nations Human Rights Council did not deem it worthwhile to condemn Equatorial Guinea, or to take any other action against this dictatorship. The nations of the African Union adhere together so tightly that they protect even the most brutal regimes, such as those in Sudan or Zimbabwe, from condemnation on the part of the United Nations. However, during my next visit to Washington in June 2009, I was invited to the U.S. State Department to describe my experiences. The fact that my conclusions were quoted in detail in a later U.S. State Department report on human rights illustrated that the Obama administration was reformulating its policies regarding Equatorial Guinea.

CHAPTER 30

Uruguay: Full Cooperation Despite Appalling Detention Conditions

At the beginning of 2009, when I met Alejandro Artucio, then Uruguayan ambassador to the United Nations in Geneva, a good friend and human rights activist who had himself suffered at the hands of the military dictatorship in the 1970s, he said to me: "We are pleased that you wish to visit Uruguay. We are aware that detention conditions are poor but we are striving to improve them. Please be as critical as you possibly can. What we need is an objective and critical external assessment of the situation with clear recommendations so that pressure can be brought to bear and the necessary measures can be implemented. Our authorities will cooperate with you in every way."

It is in this spirit that cooperation was extended to us during the entire mission, from prison directors to Interior Minister Daisy Lilian Tourne Valdez and Vice President of the Republic Rodolfo Nin Novoa. President Tabare Vazquez was in China on a state visit in March 2009 when I visited Uruguay, but he issued a directive to implement my recommendations immediately upon his return.

The United Nations country team in Montevideo was extremely cooperative, notably the director Pablo Mandeville, his human rights adviser Silvia da Rin Pagnetto, and the children's rights expert and former United Nations Special Rapporteur Juan-Miguel Petit. I had a well-rehearsed team made up of Julia Kozma, Isabelle Tschan (BIM), the outstanding interpreter Roger Kaminker, with whom the new members dovetailed very well: Claudia de la Fuente from Geneva, the forensic medical expert Maximo Duque from Colombia, and the very experienced and discreet United Nations security officer Enrique Martinel.

Silvia and Juan-Miguel asked if they could accompany us on some of the visits to prisons. Naturally, we had no problem with this at all and they joined us on all of the visits, becoming full-fledged members of our team. By the end of the mission they were as shocked as I was about the alarming conditions in the prisons, although Juan-Miguel was from Uruguay and was already quite familiar with the poor conditions of the places of detention for minors.

The Libertad Prison

We found very few classic cases of torture used to extract confessions or information. In the "Colonia Berro" juvenile prison, 50 km outside Montevideo, the young offenders were locked up in their cells most of the time, understandably causing rebellions, which were countered with brute force. The range of disciplinary measures included beatings and prison sentences, which fostered a further escalation of violence. Even so, I would not qualify such cases of violence as torture. I believe there is a significant difference between a situation where people are detained and powerless and are willfully beaten in order to extract a confession, and one where beatings are ultimately an expression of the powerlessness of a system because management has failed and can come up with nothing other than beatings to stem the escalating violence.

On the other hand, the conditions in the two largest prisons of the country, "Comcar" and "Libertad," could only be described as torture. This situation represents torture owing to the years of omission and neglect to ensure a dignified detention regime geared toward the reintegration of convicted offenders. The slow-moving and obsolescent justice system resorted to locking away more and more people in order to counter rising crime rates, resulting in a near collapse of these two prisons.

The prison with the telling name "Libertad," apparently not for cynical reasons because it is situated near a village with the same name, was already notorious at the time of the military dictatorship. Countless political prisoners were severely and systematically tortured in the factory-like main building known as "Celdario" or the smaller adjacent structure called "La Isla," reported at the time in numerous concluding observations by the United Nations Human Rights Committee among other sources. Notwithstanding the historically calamitous symbolism, Libertad still operates today as the prison with the most draconian security measures in the country. It is populated by especially dangerous recidivists and detainees who have escaped from other prisons or have been involved in uprisings.

Those who are sent to Libertad know that this is the bottom rung of the prison hierarchy and that it is going to take a very long time to work their way back up. During the five months preceding our visit, the population of this prison had grown from 589 to 1,176 detainees, of which 341 were convicted criminals and the overwhelming majority were pretrial detainees. Contrary to international minimum standards, there was no segregation between convicted and remand prisoners. The mere fact that these individuals had been sent here was interpreted by the prison management as proof that they were guilty, which of course meant that giving them a different level of treatment was pointless.

Most of the detainees were housed in the five-story Celdario brick building, in prison cells for one to three detainees. Inmates were permitted to spend a maximum of four hours per week outside their cells. The rest of the time they were locked in their cells. Even convicted criminals had no access to any type of employment, training, sports or recreational activities, which, as is known, would have been essential for their reintegration and social rehabilitation needs. Silvia, the head of the human rights section of the United Nations' country team in Uruguay, an Italian national married to a Uruguayan, asked me to open cell number 539. I did so and interviewed the detainees in that cell. While I was busy, she inspected the cell very carefully and tried to imagine what it would be like to be locked up in this cell for many years. It turned out that it was in this very cell that her husband had been detained and brutally tortured by the military in the 1970s for his political views. She was crying when we left the building.

The "Las Latas" Metal Containers

The worst conditions of all were in "Las Latas." This section of Libertad consisted of metal containers that had been delivered by a U.S. firm in 2003 and set up as a temporary solution to the prison's overcrowding. Each container was intended for one person and was equipped with a bed, table and chair, a toilet, and a sink. Originally the containers were probably even air-conditioned, which meant these cells were fairly luxurious. However, the makeshift solution had turned into a permanent facility. The air conditioning and the wastewater sewer had long since failed and the water supply worked sporadically, so detainees resorted to drinking from the toilet bowls. In the summer when the sun beat down on these metal boxes, 60 degree Centigrade temperatures inside were not uncommon, as we were plausibly assured. Instead of one person, two or three had to share each of these metal cells. The containers were arranged in four squares. The square-shaped concrete slabs were boxed in on three sides by containers laid out side by side and stacked on two levels. The fourth side included the entrance and rooms for prison staff. A metal grate instead of a roof covered the entire square facility. The containers all had a door and a peep/ventilation slit, which looked out onto the inner courtyard. There were no windows.

When we entered one of the quadrangles, we saw a young fellow who was sweeping away feces that had oozed out of ruptured plastic bags onto the dusty, dirty courtyard. Since the toilets were not functional, detainees had to use plastic bags, which they then tossed into the inner courtyard, where they burst open. The filth and stench were indescribable and the noise deafening. When the detainees became aware of our presence, they had begun to yell and beat on the metal walls of their containers, making as much noise as possible. The noise level made it impossible for us to talk, so we had to go back outside in order to discuss how we might carry out orderly interviews under such circumstances.

The prison staff seemed to have resigned themselves to all of this. When we asked the wardens if the noise was because of us, they replied that it was a daily occurrence. We approached the individual containers, first establishing contact from outside in order to communicate with individual detainees. We noticed that many of the containers had blood running down the outside metal wall from the peep slits. The desperate detainees explained that self-inflicted injuries were the only way to get the guards to respond if someone needed medical attention or had some other urgent request. The air in the containers was so stuffy, because of the overcrowding, and the absence of windows or a working ventilation system, that inmates took turns positioning themselves in front of the peep slits in order to breathe.

These detainees were also allowed a maximum of four hours outside their dungeons. Words cannot describe the detainees' anger and despair. We also thought it was inhuman for the guards to have to work in such a context of structural violence. The interim prison director, however, was of the same view as the director of prison administration of Uruguay who was present during this visit, which was that the detainees in this prison were the worst criminals in the country and they deserved no better. During my concluding discussion with the government in Montevideo, I demanded that the inhuman Las Latas metal containers be closed down immediately.

Detention Conditions in Comcar

The conditions of detention in the Santiago Vazquez ("Comcar") prison in Montevideo were not much better. However, the director of the prison at least was unapologetic and did not attempt to justify the conditions or to gloss over anything. The first thing he said to us when he greeted us was that he was completely aware that the prisons of Uruguay were dreadful. Comcar, with a capacity of 1,600, is the largest prison. In fact, when we visited the prison there were 2,768 detainees in a number of different modules, once again with no separation between convicted criminals and pretrial detainees. The director himself explained that the high incidence of violence and numerous other structural problems were attributable to the overcrowding but also to the shortage of staff and the corruption of some of the officials who smuggled drugs into the prison. It was evident that he went to great pains to allow detainees greater freedom where possible. Detainee representatives, elected by their peers in each module, affirmed that this director was the best one they had ever had.

With the exception of high-security module two, the rule in this prison is open detention, which means that the cells were open from 0900 to 1800 and the detainees were free to move about in the individual modules. The condition of the buildings, sanitary facilities, and structural violence meant that these congested modules were simply inhuman and intolerable, and I once again requested that the worst modules be closed down.

The detainees obligingly helped us as we felt our way in the darkness along the corridors, avoiding the holes in the floor so as not to tumble into the open sewage pipe below. Our detainee/guides pointed out crumbling walls that seemed on the verge of collapsing, and everywhere there were rats scampering between the cells. The inmates were visibly pleased that someone was showing interest in their problems and complaints. At the same time, I felt there was an underlying rage and disposition to violence. It occurred to me that a mere spark could unleash a firestorm.

Toward the end of our visit we noticed that a number of detainees in module 5 had suddenly started a fight, which escalated swiftly. The module was immediately locked down and searched and the director showed us an impressive collection of self-made knives, which could certainly cause a lot of harm. Although the visiting hours had just begun, the director declared that they were over because of the security breach, which merely added fuel to the fire. We had observed how carefully the detainees had prepared to receive their wives and partners, how they had quarreled over the limited water available for showers, and fashioned makeshift tents with blankets in the courtyard to create a little privacy. These visits were the only bright spot during the dreary everyday life in prison. When the angry relatives got wind of the fact that our group was in the director's office for a concluding discussion, they surrounded the office and urged me to mediate in the dispute and reverse this collective punishment. Following some loud and emotional negotiations we managed to de-escalate the tense situation.

Implemented Recommendations

Despite my scathing criticism of the conditions of detention, the government kept its promise and was extremely cooperative and willing to take my recommendations seriously and actually implement them. A few days after my departure, President Tabare Vazquez personally issued a directive to close down the sections in the two prisons as I had requested and to make available a number of army barracks, appropriately adapted, as swing space for detainees until a modern prison could be built. Some time later I heard that he had also dismissed his internal affairs minister.

The great willingness of the government under President José Mujica to combat torture and improve the situation of detainees was demonstrated in the extension of an official invitation to implement the Atlas of Torture project in 2012. It was a special experience for me to meet President Mujica in his modest office and to discuss with him his personal experience, as former leader of the Tupamaros guerrilla movement, of having been detained during the military dictatorship in a small hole for thirteen years and having been exposed to particularly brutal torture methods. Although this was the time when several military and civilian leaders of the dictatorship were brought to justice for the crimes they had committed some forty years ago, "Pepe" Mujica showed no feelings of revenge and was open to genuine reconciliation. During our first assessment visit to the country, I was able to visit some of the prisons again and, while I witnessed improvements, overcrowding and inhuman conditions of detention remained a serious problem that could only be solved by comprehensive and systematic reforms of the criminal justice system. In this respect my project team, consisting of Tiphanie Crittin and Moritz Birk, arrived at a crucial moment when a prison law reform was on the way and an independent NPM was about to be set up to carry out systematic monitoring of all places of detention.

The project, together with its local partner SERPAJ, intervened on different levels: By supporting the reform of the new prison law with a concrete legal proposal and holding regular meetings with high-level officials to consult on and advocate for the necessary legal and institutional changes. Mindful of the slow pace of large-scale reforms, the project also intervened on a grassroots level by developing a guide for prisoners on *Defending Yourself from Inside Prison*. The guide was widely disseminated and used for training in numerous facilities throughout the country. While the work on reforming the criminal justice system is far from being completed, the project has advanced the urgently needed debate on the rights of detainees and contributed to crucial changes. It is hoped that the country, with the help of its new NPM and the many highly professional and committed civil society organizations, continues on its promising path.

CHAPTER 31

Kazakhstan: Potemkin Villages

The five Central Asian republics are not exactly regarded as shining examples of democracy and human rights. In Uzbekistan my predecessor, Theo van Boven, established the existence of systematic torture, and the situation in Turkmenistan is so bad that international human rights monitors are hardly allowed into the country at all. On the other hand, Kazakhstan makes skillful attempts to improve its reputation through cooperation with independent experts, and through a policy of rapprochement with European organizations such as the Council of Europe. Profiting from petroleum wealth, in 2010 Kazakh diplomacy even succeeded in taking over the chairmanship of the Organization for Security and Cooperation in Europe (OSCE), headquartered in Vienna's Hofburg Palace.

Exemplary Official Cooperation

Cooperation on the part of Kazakh authorities during my mission in May 2009 was downright exemplary. My team included the forensic medical expert Duarte Vieira, Isabelle Tschan and Roland Schmidt from the BIM, plus Birgit Kainz Labbé (Geneva), who had earlier worked for the OSCE in Kazakhstan and still had access to the very best contacts. We had unrestricted access to all the institutions that we wanted to visit: prisons, police lockups, secret service detention facilities, psychiatric hospitals, and special detention centers for children, juveniles, and immigrants.

In Soviet times the inhospitable nature of the Kazakh steppes, with their enormous temperature extremes, played an important role in the far-ranging Gulag system. Especially noteworthy is the region of the industrial city

Karaganda, where fourteen prisons that are still in use tell the tale of how many people were incarcerated during that era. Thanks to the relative wealth of this country it has been possible to invest a great deal of money in the renovation of old prisons. For that reason I found the prison conditions to be better than in many other ex-Soviet states, such as Georgia and Moldova.

Torture by the police, as well as mistreatment in prisons, still occurs, but I was unable to detect any widespread or systematic practice of these. Only in certain institutions such as detention centers for children or juveniles (CVIARN) in Karaganda did corporal punishment and beatings seem to be routine.

Children's Prisons

However, the Kazakhs were true masters at showing me "Potemkin Villages." It was clear that they had carefully prepared for my visit. For instance, the fifty-six children and juveniles between three (!) and eighteen years of age that we encountered in the above-mentioned CVIARN were so well prepared in what they should say to me that the skills of a detective were required to get to the truth through their wall of silence and rehearsed lies. The director told us about regular volleyball games and similar sports activities in the open air, which upon further investigation proved to be completely fabricated. All the children seemed extremely withdrawn and fearful—even the smallest, whether they had been brought there through arrest for juvenile crimes, or because they had lost their parents, or because they had been picked up as street children. All of their heads had been shaved. No one was willing to talk about beatings or mistreatment. Our suspicions were aroused when we noticed that all of them were serving up the exact same story about their days full of sports, their excellent food, and their kindly treatment at the hands of their "educators." It became clear to us that the tale about daily volleyball could not be true when we asked the director to show us the court. There was indeed a sports field in the open air, but it was so overgrown that it was quite obvious that no one had played volleyball there for months. This placed all the other claims under suspicion.

When, in individual interviews, we asked the youngsters directly about mistreatment, we noticed that some of them became very reticent. They fearfully looked around for hidden cameras. However, eventually we were able to convince them that we were conducting undisturbed and unobserved conversations. Then the truth came gushing out, namely that they were being routinely beaten, something which was, in the end, confirmed by forensic investigation. After exacting investigations we were able to detect similar corporal punishment in Colony 155/6, the juvenile detention facility in Almaty. And in Astana's investigatory holding prison (SIZO EC-166/1) every single one of more than seven hundred inmates had been carefully instructed about what to say and what not to say. Never had I seen such painstaking preparation for my visit in any other country.

Staged Plays

And yet, the Potemkin Village effect did not consist solely of exact instructions to the inmates about what to say to us. The government had gone to great expense to put on genuine stage productions for us. In the Arshaly prison (EC-166/5), a prison band was even founded in our honor. This band was so abruptly slapped together that the various instruments did not really work together, but the inmates nonetheless gamely tried to entertain us with their music. The prison management had apparently not realized that we, in candid conversations with inmates, would quickly find out that this prison band had not been in existence for very long at all, but had, rather, just recently been formed to impress us. Naturally we asked the prison director to keep this particular group in place after our departure, as one means of improving prison conditions.

Also quite transparent was the attempt to inform us that the dark solitary confinement cells, which served to "quarantine" new inmates and to discipline problem inmates, had not been in use for quite a long time. It was true that all of these cells were empty when we arrived. But they still smelled strongly of urine, sweat, and other typical prison odors. Moreover, fresh remains of meals were strewn about. So we asked to see the register for the solitary confinement cells. Unfortunately for the prison directorate this register was carefully maintained, and it was quite a while before we finally got to see it. That was because the officials had to quickly remove from the register all of the inmates who had been released from solitary confinement shortly before the security services announced our arrival. And, in orderly fashion, they even wrote down the very date of our arrival as precisely the date of all of these releases from solitary confinement. As an example, there were exact entries that someone just one day before had been sentenced to a disciplinary punishment of two weeks of solitary confinement, but then the following day was released, along with all of the other inmates, for no apparent reason. Nonetheless, the prison directorate insisted that all of this was perfectly orderly, and naturally had nothing to do with our visit.

All of this led to our decision to interview all of the inmates who were released from solitary confinement on the day of our visit. Needless to say, they were very pleasantly surprised that they were all released at the same time in the course of an afternoon, for no particular reason, and were even told to clean their cells and to disappear as quickly as possible. Of course they came to understand the correlation with our arrival, and thanked us heartily for this unexpected reprieve. They told us that in the last few days the entire prison had been painted white, in the greatest haste. And in fact, we had to be very careful not to lean on any wall or door, because the paint was still wet. Even the barbed wire fences had been whitewashed and looked quite smart.

In the meantime, the head of Kazakh penal authority himself arrived from Astana, so during the concluding conversations with the prison director we joked that it was not necessary to make such a fuss about us. We would discover all the deception anyway. In the end he himself had to laugh over the matter of the prison band. Not really a bad idea at all, he said, by way of patting himself on the back, so to speak. He attempted to flatter me by pointing out that if we ourselves were to welcome such honored guests, we would surely do an equivalent amount of cleanup and straightening. After all, it wasn't every day that his prison underwent a UN inspection.

Party in the Prison Yard?

We found the most beautiful Potemkin Village in the women's prison in Koksu. That day we got into our UN vehicles and departed Astana early, then went off in the direction of Karaganda, all of which the security officials who were always watching us were bound to report to their colleagues in Karaganda. Before long a police car with blue lights flashing came up and turned around in front of us. The officers told us to follow them. Apparently, such a high delegation as ours could not be allowed to drive around in Kazakhstan without a police escort! In order to at least keep up the appearance of unannounced visits, we took the next exit and made an unplanned visit to various police stations in the industrial city of Temirtau. Our police escort must have considered us to be very rude guests indeed. But in turn the detour cost us quite a bit of time, which we would then be short of in Karaganda.

We had selected the women's prison as the last prison to visit for the day, but it was situated so far outside of the city, and was so hard to find, that it was already dusk when we arrived. The director had become worried that we were not going to come, and even sent out a car. We allowed that car to show us the way, although we felt a little embarrassed about it. The director greeted us like old friends who were arriving late to a get-together that had been arranged long before. I must have seemed a little silly when I apologized for our late arrival. He seemed somewhat impatient, and immediately began a tour of the prison at a fast clip.

Although it was late in the evening, all of the inmates were gathered in a large meadow having a party. Western pop music was blaring loudly out of huge loudspeakers, and the women were eager to show us various dance steps. The director hastened to explain to us that the inmates organized parties like this every day. And he wanted to continue in that vein. He was so caught up in the task of showing everything to us personally that it was difficult to explain to him that now we wanted to have conversations with the inmates. He seemed to be nearly insulted when we explained to him that he would not be allowed to be present during these conversations.

Naturally the deception evaporated with the first interview. We were told that the whole music setup had been brought in and installed just a few days before. Especially conspicuous were the freshly ironed bright white sheets on the beds in the large dormitories. A woman told us that these sheets had arrived four days ago. And since all the beds were so beautifully made up, all were told that they must sleep on the floor until further notice. Now at last I understood why the director was somewhat impatient. Someone must have told him that we would be coming to his prison right at the beginning of our mission in Kazakhstan. He had prepared everything, and then it was four whole days before we finally arrived! I was glad that at least the women would once again be able to spend the night in their beds, and, moreover, in beds that were now so nicely made up, fresh and clean.

CHAPTER 32

Jamaica: Structural Violence Instead of Torture

"Island in the sun" is what Harry Belafonte once fondly called this Caribbean island in the song of the same name. Indeed, if you are gently swinging in a hammock with a glass of Jamaican rum in your hand and Bob Marley's "No Woman No Cry" in your ear, gazing at one of the pearl white beaches of Montego Bay, you could be forgiven for imagining you are on heaven's doorstep. You would have no idea that in the Freeport police station on the other end of town there are people who have not seen the Jamaican sun for many years because they are in detention, although they have not been convicted by any court of law. These people were arrested by the police solely on suspicion of having committed a criminal offense. Because the cells in pretrial detention facilities are overcrowded, pretrial detainees who do not have the money to buy their release are simply left to rot in the police custody cells, most of them forgotten by the rest of the world. A few days before our arrival in February 2010, a detainee uprising was brutally quelled in the Horizon Remand Center in Kingston.

The "Freeport" Police Station in Montego Bay

Along with experienced members like Julia Kozma (BIM) ad Derrick Pounder, my team also included Claudia de la Fuente, who had joined the Geneva team fairly recently but had already accompanied me on my visit to Uruguay; Tiphanie Crittin, who joined the BIM team as a Swiss expert (after Isabelle Tschan left) and passed her "baptism by fire" in Jamaica with flying colors. Two experienced United Nations staff from Jamaica, Lincoln Campbell and Hayley Brooks, came along for our security.

When we visited "Freeport" on 20 February 2010, we discovered 159 detainees crammed into a small space. The place of detention consisted of a long corridor flanked by cells. The first six cells contained women and children. A little light filtered through to these cells. The men's cells were separated from these cells by a locked door with a wire mesh grille. The further along the corridor we went, the darker, hotter, and stuffier it became. The stench was almost intolerable. When we turned on our flashlights we saw cockroaches and other vermin everywhere. The noise level was so high that it was difficult to speak with individual detainees in their cells. Fearing reprisals, few agreed to leave their cells for an interview.

The atmosphere was electric and violent. We felt that all it would take was a spark to detonate an explosion of violence that would be matched with violence from the police. Practically all of the detainees described beatings and other forms of violence from other detainees and the prison guards. I tried to imagine how long I could endure such detention conditions. Probably not much longer than a few days. After that I would probably lose my mind. Yet there were people here who had been held in these absolutely inhuman conditions for more than four years. They told us that they spent most of their time doing absolutely nothing in these locked, dark, jam-packed, and stinky cells. Occasionally they were let out to go to the toilet or "shower." But the long corridor was as far as they could go, even when visitors came with food or clean clothes. Detainees could only talk to their relatives through the close-mesh wire door separating the rear section of the corridor from the front. The chief warden fully agreed with us that the detention conditions in "Freeport" were inhuman, not only for the detainees but also for the staff who worked there and were responsible for "maintaining order." However, as a small wheel in the police hierarchy he was unable to do anything about it.

Inhuman conditions of detention usually do not qualify as torture because the term "torture" requires the intentional infliction of severe pain or suffering for a specific purpose. Torture by negligence is, therefore, a contradiction in terms. Nevertheless, the situation in Freeport seemed to be different. Our conclusion was that the complete disregard for human dignity could not simply be dismissed as negligence. We could not shake the impression that the responsible officials and politicians had intentionally created such appalling conditions of detention and maintained them to serve as a deterrent or to intimidate and punish these people. I therefore urgently requested the government to immediately close down this police jail on the grounds of infringement of the prohibition of torture. As far as I know nothing has changed yet.

The May Pen Police Jail

The conditions in the May Pen police station were comparable to those in Montego Bay. The corridor in this jail was U-shaped, with the toilets and "showers" at the back, in the bend of the U. When we visited on 16 February 2010, to add to existing woes the toilets had backed up and feces were spilling out into the corridor. The detainees in the adjacent cells, which were nearly as dark as the ones in "Freeport," had wrapped their t-shirts around mouth and nose because of the stench. To make matters worse, the detainees were only allowed outside their cells twice daily in order to use the toilets, although many had the runs because of the dreadful sanitary conditions and spoiled food they were given. They had to relieve themselves into plastic bags in front of their cellmates.

A thirty-nine-year-old man was in tears as he told us that he was very ill and had been prescribed a strict diet by the doctor. Despite this, he was receiving the standard food and had the runs continuously. His cellmates had beaten him repeatedly, he added, because he was unable to wait until he was allowed to go to the toilet. The prison guards had also beaten him and scalded him with hot water. I demanded the immediate closure of the police jail in this case too, so far without success.

A Brutalized Society

Although the detention conditions in the police stations and jails in Kingston and other cities were somewhat better, the two police stations mentioned earlier were by no means isolated cases. They were the tip of the structural violence iceberg in Jamaican society and especially as regards the interaction between the police and ordinary citizens who were suspected, rightly or wrongly, of a criminal offense.

Kingston's inner city was controlled by a number of different criminal organizations, which maintained close ties to the political parties of the country. The bosses of these organizations, which specialize in the arms and drug trades, are respectfully known as "Dons" and are anything but squeamish when it comes to dealing with their rivals, uninvolved persons, or the police. We visited a few of these lords in prison in order to get a better idea about how they continue to wield power and command violence from behind bars. Anyone who has not submitted to the protection of one of these Dons would be well advised to keep a distance from the controlled areas of Kingston.

Jamaica has one of the highest per capita weapon and murder rates in the world. This may at least partially explain why the police officials' nerves are often on edge during operations against organized crime. On the other hand, the police are anything but circumspect as well, which contributes to an escalation in the violence and a further brutalization of society. Instead of detaining suspects, there has been an increasing tendency to deliberately shoot them. Hunt's Bay, near Kingston's inner city, is one of the police stations notorious for this type of deployment. The propensity for violence here is so palpable one could cut it with a knife. We experienced this ourselves when a high-ranking police officer became extremely aggressive and almost turned violent toward us merely because we were seeking more detailed information about a detainee who had not been recorded, was very frightened, and whom they had evidently hidden from us.

The "Horizon" Remand Prison

We also encountered a climate of violence in the prisons. On 8 February 2010, just four days before our arrival in Kingston, a rebellion had taken place at the Horizon remand prison because the water supply had been interrupted for several days. When the water was suddenly turned on, only a small number of detainees were allowed access. This infuriated the other detainees who were suffering from thirst. They smashed down a number of cell doors, freeing other detainees. A special police unit reacted with extreme brutality. Miraculously, there were no fatalities, but seventy inmates were injured, some seriously.

We interviewed the most seriously injured detainees in the infirmary of the Tower Street Prison and, with the expertise of our forensic medical expert Derrick Pounder, were able to establish that their injuries had not been caused by self-defense actions on the part of the police to counter out-of-control detainees, as the prison director tried to persuade us. Quite the contrary, the violence had targeted detainees who had tried in vain to protect themselves from the excessively violent police. The director's version lacked credibility if only for the fact that very few police officers had been injured, and those who had, had received only light injuries.

Armadale, a Juvenile Prison for Girls

On 22 May 2009, turmoil in Armadale, a juvenile prison for girls, led to seven deaths and severely burned detainees. We interviewed several of the badly traumatized survivors nine months later in the newly commissioned Diamond Crest juvenile prison for girls in Alligator Pond. In Jamaica, Armadale has become a symbol for structural violence and a lack of empathy for detainees, in this case even young offenders. The facility, like so many others, was overcrowded. In the bedroom where the turmoil took place, there were fourteen mattresses, arranged in seven pairs, for twenty-three girls. Although the open detention system was the rule here, the fact that collective punishments were meted out even for minor breaches of the prison rules meant that the girls were often locked up in their bedrooms and were prevented from taking part in their educational and leisure activities. They even had to take their meals in these crowded rooms.

Structural Violence

During our final meeting with the government I summed up the situation, explaining that torture in the classic sense, involving the extraction of a confession through the intentional infliction of pain and suffering, was not in fact an issue in Jamaica. What was problematic, however, was the sheer magnitude of structural violence in society, in places of detention and in the way the police deals with the public. One is spared the trouble of extracting a confession when suspicious persons are shot to death. When people are treated like animals and detained for years in appalling conditions in dark police cells, it is worse for the victims than being subjected to two days of torture. Again, forcibly obtaining a confession is unnecessary if individuals are held in police custody longer than the maximum sentence they could have received for the offence they are accused of having committed.

I had the impression that the authorities in Kingston, especially Security Minister Dwight Nelson and Justice Minister Dorothy Lightbourne had understood our analysis and recommendations and had agreed with them in principle. I was therefore all the more surprised by the incensed reaction of the ambassador in New York when among other things I presented my report on Jamaica at my last appearance before the United Nations General Assembly in October 2010. My critical appraisal of his country was allegedly not credible at all because I had after all, in no uncertain terms, assured the government in Kingston during my final meeting with them that torture was not a problem in Jamaica.

CHAPTER 33

Papua New Guinea: Traditional Structures Coexist with Globalization

Papua New Guinea (PNG) is a fascinating country with a wealth of different cultures, religions, and traditions. Its area of 462,000 km² is divided between the main island with its densely populated highlands and huge tracts of impassable rain forest as well as countless islands. The over six million inhabitants speak more than eight hundred different languages. Conflicts arising between families, ethnic groups, and peoples, including crimes, are settled even today by traditional village courts through mediation based on customary law. Needless to say, such conflict resolution mechanisms do not always meet twenty-first-century human rights standards, in particular in areas like gender equality. Yet their specific purpose is to uphold peace and harmony in society by agreeing to settle disputes through mutual consent. Success is not guaranteed, however, and many disputes involving land and other resources, rape, murder, and similar crimes are settled between families by resorting to violence.

As Papua New Guinea has not been spared the blessings of civilization, these disputes are no longer settled with bows and arrows but with firearms. As a result, violence and organized crime have increased enormously. The capital, Port Moresby, is now among the most dangerous cities in the world. For my mission in May 2010, the United Nations hired a security company for our protection, which meant that we had to travel everywhere in convoy. My well-rehearsed team included Claudia de la Fuente, Christina Saunders, and Mathilde Bogner (OHCHR), Roland Schmidt and Tiphanie Crittin (BIM), our medical forensic expert Duarte Vieira, and our two interpreters, Mathew Nelson and Monica Pallus.

Kup Women for Peace

In the highlands, altercations involving weapons between neighboring peoples and families cause far more deaths nowadays than in the past. In Kup, a small, remote mountain village not far from Kundiawa, we observed how the women of the feuding peoples had launched a joint initiative aimed at ending the senseless spiral of violence and revenge through a peace initiative involving mediation. The peace lasted almost a decade and this exemplary initiative ("Kup Women for Peace") became a model for other women's associations.

Just before our visit in May 2010, the men had picked up their weapons again and destroyed all of the joint buildings, institutions, and fields that the women had painstakingly built up. All that remained for us to see were the ruins of what had been jointly constructed by the women, and their sadness was palpable. In spite of all this the women had begun a new peace initiative, this time aimed at bringing together the village elders and leaders on both sides to a large meadow in Kup for a discussion. While the women were pleading with the men to finally put a stop to the senseless violence, the men seemed to have nothing better to do than to blame each other's side for the new escalation in violence. When I asked if the police could be approached to provide assistance, the response was a baffled shaking of the head. The police had never even been seen in this remote area and in any case would never agree to become involved in a dispute of this nature.

Sorcery

Another tradition that gives rise to a number of human rights problems in PNG is best described as "black magic" or "sorcery." A visibly shaken and frightened man told us the following story, which allegedly also took place in a small, remote village in the highlands.

A man, with whom the storyteller had had a long-standing dispute over the ownership of a plot of land, suddenly died in their village. The man and his wife were accused by the family of the deceased man of having killed him by means of supernatural powers. The decision reached by the village assembly was that the reason for the sudden, unexpected death of the man could only be determined with the help of a well-known "grand sorceress" from another village. In the meantime, the two accused were under house arrest.

Upon arrival, the magician consulted with the village elders. Our interlocutor maintained that she had fallen into a trance after drinking home-brewed beer prepared by the village elders and the family of the deceased. Around midnight and in a state of trance, she declared to the people of the village that the accused couple had caused the death of the man in question by means of supernatural powers. This verdict meant the lynch law was to be applied, and the two were handed over to the angry mob. In front of their children they were dragged out of their house, severely abused, taken outside the village, hung by their feet from a large tree, and left alone to die slowly and agonizingly. Whereas his wife did not survive the torture, the man was freed on the third day by an unfamiliar woman and, mustering his last bit of strength, managed to flee through the forest and into the valley, where he was picked up and tended to by a humanitarian organization. Although he was terribly worried about his underage children, he did not dare return to his village. He was certain that the family of the deceased had accused him of committing the murder by summoning supernatural powers because they wanted to appropriate the disputed plot of land.

The Role of the Police

Although I was not certain I could fully believe the man's story, human rights organizations assured us emphatically that it was not an isolated case. On the contrary, they stressed that the overwhelming majority of murders and cases of torture in Papua New Guinea were linked to sorcery. In an orderly rule-of-law state, the police are supposed to protect people, such as the ones in the story we were told, from such issues as accusations of sorcery, but here the police deliberately stay out of conflicts and rituals involving traditional village justice. Moreover, grand sorcerers and sorceresses were very highly regarded in PNG and the police had no desire to tangle with them, as confirmed to us by a number of police chiefs we met in the highlands.

The only role the police could play in these situations was to take into police custody for protection purposes people who were accused or were being pursued. For example, we found three men in a small police station in Arawa, in the south of the autonomous island of Bougainville, who had already spent several weeks in a cell. They explained that they were in the cell of their own free will and for their protection because it was the only place where they felt safe. They had no idea how long they were going to stay. All three had been accused of murder by means of supernatural powers (poisoning) by the relatives of deceased persons.

In one of the cases, a three-member court had even acquitted the accused of the murder charge on the basis of a medical report stating that the victim had died from complications of diabetes. All the same, the relatives of the deceased person were still after the fellow with machetes and bows and arrows. He had asked the police to arrest the relatives of the deceased who were pursuing him, but the police chief of Arawa explained to us that there were so many cases of sorcery in the villages that the police simply did not have the manpower or other resources (e.g., vehicles) to address them all. The police chief pointed out that he was already helping considerably by making his cells available for protection purposes.

Human Rights–Based Duty to Protect

We spent a good deal of time as a team discussing how such cases should be assessed from a human rights angle and whether as special rapporteur on torture I should adopt a position. It is beyond doubt that people accused of sorcery often are abused in the most cruel way and/or murdered. It is also clear that these cases are not few and far between but that this practice is very widespread both in the highlands and on the islands. I had various conversations with potential victims and perpetrators on the subject of sorcery in twenty-first-century PNG. I could not shake the suspicion that it was often being used as a pretext to cleverly dispose of disagreeable adversaries with trumped up charges of crimes committed by means of supernatural powers. I believe therefore that accusations of sorcery, as well as the substantiation of such allegations by "grand sorcerers," should be punishable as criminal offenses and therefore should be pursued as such by the police. On the other hand, a number of anthropologists, sociologists, and human rights experts who are familiar with this phenomenon agree that people in PNG still strongly believe in sorcery. Further, they are agreed that "grand sorcerers," who hold respected positions in society, are ascribed clairvoyant powers and the ability to tell if a person has used supernatural powers to murder someone or cause pain and suffering such as a serious illness.

In any case, such a "verdict" should never lead to torture and lynch law, and the state has a human rights responsibility to protect victims in this respect. If a state evades this human rights duty to protect, it is guilty of torture by omission.

Inasmuch as the traditional customary law criminal justice administered by village courts in PNG is explicitly recognized along with the ordinary criminal justice administered by state courts, the result is a blending of the two. In cases involving sorcery, it is often not entirely clear if a village court has handed down a "verdict" or if victims have had an offense "transferred" to them by a "grand sorcerer" for "punishment" by members of the injured families. At any rate the police avoid getting involved, as such matters are not for the state security forces since they have neither the necessary resources nor expertise to handle them.

Police Brutality

The police (Royal Papua New Guinea Constabulary) are indeed in a very sorry state. At the time of our mission in May 2010 there were no more than 1,200 police officers in service for the entire country. Officers are poorly trained, badly paid, and known for their brutality. We found no cases of severe torture involving cleverly devised methods of extracting confessions. But when people are detained and in police custody, they are routinely beaten, severely, with wooden sticks, iron bars, machetes, or fan belts, just to show detainees who is in charge.

While we were interviewing detainees in the cells of the relatively sizeable police station in Buka, a high-ranking security officer from Port Moresby suddenly appeared and not only shouted at us very aggressively but also physically attacked our medical doctor, Duarte Vieira. We barely managed to de-escalate this dangerous situation through intense diplomatic efforts.

When detainees attempt to escape from prison, they can expect harsh treatment as well. For instance, on 13 April 2010, a total of eighty-four inmates broke out of the Mount Hagen prison, of which twenty-three were recaptured. We interviewed them in their disciplinary cells. Security forces had beaten every single one of them severely, and had also used a variety of other methods to inflict further pain and suffering, namely: shots fired at short range, burns using hot machetes, and severed Achilles heels. They were locked up afterward in the disciplinary cells without any form of medical attention.

Violence Against Women

These and similar incidents certainly do not increase the trust of the population in their police force. Although domestic violence against women and children is an everyday occurrence, few women would think of going to the police in such cases. Apart from the fact that they could hardly expect any form of assistance to protect them from their violent spouses, they would run the risk of being detained, beaten, or raped by the police. The situation in the Mount Hagen police lockup was especially bad. Most of the female inmates seemed to have been detained in order to do the officers' laundry, to clean the cells of the male detainees, and to perform sexual favors for the officers and the male inmates. The unanimous complaints from all of the female inmates and a few male inmates appeared to be substantiated when we discovered a large number of unused condoms in the police chief's office.

Private Security Services

The combination of minimal confidence by the population in police protection and very high levels of violence in society leads to the hiring of private security services by those able to afford it. The London-based private security company G4S alone had 4,800 well-trained and relatively professional security staff in Papua New Guinea, which was four times as many as the Royal PNG Constabulary staff. The employees of private security companies also earn far more than the police. It is not surprising that the ambitious and better-trained among the police are enticed away by private security companies, while within the police force, motivation and morale are very low. According to Tom Kolunga, deputy commander of the PNG police at the time of our visit, approximately 50 percent of all police officers were either out sick or unfit for duty for other reasons.

Globalization as a Threat to Traditional Vital Structures

In addition to everything else, Papua New Guinea has substantial reserves of natural materials such as tropical timber, minerals, and oil, which are being exploited by multinationals with complete disregard for traditional structures and cultures. On the island of Bougainville, resistance against the exploitation of a large copper mine in Panguna by indigenous people even led to an armed conflict, the closure of the mine in 1989, and finally to an autonomous status for the island in 2002.

The construction of a pipeline and exploitation of the enormous natural gas reserves by Exxon/Mobil and other multinationals exacerbated the social tensions in the country significantly, as violent demonstrations have already indicated. The police appear to be inadequately prepared for the clash of traditional structures with the economic forces of globalization. It is difficult to predict what this will mean for the future. In my report, I have called for a fundamental reform of the Royal Papua New Guinea Constabulary as a particularly urgent measure. Coping with the upheavals in this fascinating country without resorting to violence is going to require much more than this measure.

CHAPTER 34

Greece: The Joint Asylum and Migration
Policy of the European Union, Put to the Test

In October 2010, my last official mission took me to Greece. I was accompanied there by a comparatively new team. Sonia Cronin (Geneva) and Moritz Birk (BIM) were on a mission with me for the first time, but Tiphanie Crittin had already gathered a lot of experience during the far more difficult missions to Jamaica and Papua New Guinea. I was especially glad that I would be accompanied by Duarte Vieira (despite his full calendar as president of the most important international organization of forensic experts) on this my last, and for him already the seventh, mission. Above all, we intended to pay special attention to the state of affairs of refugees and irregular migrants. That was the case because in Greece, more than in any other country, the consequences of a failed "common" European Asylum and Migration Policy were already apparent.

Fortress Europe

Spurred on by a xenophobic populist right-wing campaign, the politicians of Europe after the fall of the Iron Curtain reduced to a minimum the legal immigration of workers, a type of immigration that, shortly before, had been furthered as a purposeful recruitment policy to boost the economy. That led to a situation where many of those desiring to migrate as workers switched over to the asylum approach. This was preferable because international refugee law provides that those seeking asylum can have temporary right of residence until such time as the legal process decides whether or not they are refugees according to the 1951 Geneva Refugee Convention. For the most part, the number of asylum officials was not up to the task of handling the rapid rise in the number of asylum-seekers, and the huge backlog led to the existence of a procedural period of several years. That was advantageous primarily to a certain group of people: those who in the course of the asylum process integrated themselves to such an extent that they managed to overstay their asylum period quite unnoticed, and remained in their new country of residence.

Instead of accelerating the asylum process through the necessary increase in personnel, so that misuse of the asylum process would no longer pay off, the European states began, step by step, to make access to Europe and to a fair asylum procedure, as well as refugee protection, more difficult. This made the process impossible for genuine refugees as well. All of this brought organized crime into the picture. Those who genuinely need protection from persecution in their home country, and wish to be recognized as refugees in Europe, often have no other choice but to sell all that they have to unscrupulous smugglers who make a business out of exploiting such people, and who smuggle them into Europe in various audacious ways fraught with danger. As part of these schemes, the smugglers treat the refugees to outlandish stories about their future lives in Europe. If these people really knew what awaited them in Europe they would never go through the trouble and expense of traveling there. As was true during the Cold War, most Europeans no longer differentiate between refugees deserving of asylum (as with the solidarity shown during the 1956 Hungary crisis or the 1968 Prague Spring) and migrant workers whose immigration must be regulated.

Foreigners are foreigners, and that means "illegals" for most people, and unfortunately also for the authorities. In order to defend "Fortress Europe" against "an alien tide," European politicians initiated ever more restrictiveness. Since interior borders have gone for the benefit of the common market, an "area of freedom, justice and security" has been created for the citizens of the European Union, and the joint external borders of this realm have to be defended against irregular migration by specially trained military and police officials of the European frontier defense force called "Frontex."

Instead of conceptualizing a true common European Asylum and Migration Policy for the twenty-first century oriented toward demographic development, and allowing a degree of legal immigration, European politics tended toward the so-called Florian Principle: Out of considerations of humanitarianism and international law, genuine refugees must in the end be granted refuge in Europe, but not in our country please! That is the spirit of the original

Dublin Accord of 1990, which was recast in the so-called Dublin Regulations after 2000. Wherever refugees first set foot on European Union soil, there they should remain to await the outcome of their asylum case. It is considered irrelevant whether the refugees speak German, English, or French, or perhaps have relatives or friends in Sweden, the Netherlands, or Austria who could help alleviate the difficult lot that is existence as a refugee. What would come of it if the refugees could only choose their country of asylum!

Austrian politicians found the Dublin system exceptionally unfair as long as Austria had a long external EU border with the Czech Republic, Slovakia, Hungary, and Slovenia, and made a special effort to send its military to defend against irregular migration on the border. The gendarmerie and border defense posts of Austria equipped with infrared cameras to defend the "Green Border" at Gmünd or the "Blue Border" at Marchegg were, in the end, fully overtaxed. Such was the case each night when the gendarmes or soldiers picked up soaked and exhausted refugees from Afghanistan, Pakistan, or Chechnya whom unscrupulous smugglers had left out in the Bohemian forest or in boats on the River March.

Border "Defense"

I was often present at these nighttime activities, in my capacity as the head of the northern Lower Austria visiting committee of the Interior Ministry's Human Rights Advisory Council. The officials showed us how, as they sat in warm buses equipped with night vision and infrared equipment, they could recognize, there in the night, "illegals" who had been left alone in the Bohemian forest without documents. I remember how shocked I was when in the year 2000 the gendarmerie officials in Gänserndorf proudly showed us an Interior Ministry propaganda-instruction film in which "illegals" were detected in the night by helicopters. With night vision equipment, from the cockpit of the helicopter one could distinctly observe how a family with children fearfully hid in a ditch by the road, to protect themselves from a presumed attack from the helicopter. In the end this Pakistani refugee family was captured by the brave gendarmes and turned over to the authorities. I don't really know what the point of this film was, but it reminded me of war.

If these people had been caught before they set foot on Austrian soil they would have been turned over to Czech or Slovakian border authorities. Whether they were then sent back to Pakistan or Chechnya was no concern of ours. However, if they made it over the border, generally they presented themselves voluntarily to the gendarmerie and enunciated the word "asylum." Then the Austrian authorities were obliged to first take them to a makeshift gendarmerie detention center on the border and provide them with food, hot tea, and warm clothing, and then to identify them as far as possible, and subsequently to send them to an initial intake camp for refugees in Traiskirchen. Even if these people really wanted to go to Germany, Sweden, Italy, or England, Austria was obliged to carry out the asylum process and provide for these "illegals," a stipulation most Austrian gendarmes and politicians at that time regarded as utterly unfair.

If the refugees were clever enough to pass through Austria unnoticed and reach Germany or Italy, and were picked up by the authorities there, on the basis of the Dublin system, Austria would be obliged to take them back, and then to watch over them during the asylum process so well that they would not be able to "flee" again to Germany, even if, say, they had relatives there. Naturally this system led to more and more asylum applicants being placed in deportation detention.

All of that is in the past, and nearly forgotten. In the meantime all of our Eastern neighbors have joined the European Union and the "Schengen area." The external EU border is no longer to be defended against irregular migration in Austria, but rather in Poland, Slovakia, Bulgaria, Spain, Italy, or Greece. Refugees can now legally apply for asylum in Austria only when they can afford to arrive by air with a valid visa.

Any Chechen refugees who make it to Austria over the land route through Ukraine, Poland, and the Czech Republic with the aid of smugglers can be sent back to where they came from. All we need to do is employ the European fingerprint databank "Eurodac" and prove that they actually first set foot on EU soil in Poland. The same goes for Afghan refugees who made their way through Iran and Turkey to Greece. It is no longer our problem if they have been traumatized by their difficult, torturous flight and desperately need our protection, or if they cannot really get a fair asylum hearing in Poland or Greece, or are sent back to their country of origin. If the Austrian authorities find their fingerprints in the Eurodac database, a very abbreviated Dublin Procedure takes place, and the bewildered people find themselves sitting in a bus or plane to Warsaw or Athens. Soon after the EU accession of our Central and Eastern European neighbor countries, I, along with other members of our commission of the Human Rights Advisory Council, again visited fairly lonely police outposts on the borders with the Czech Republic and Slovakia. We found no more detainees but police officers who now seemed very satisfied with the Dublin system.

Only Thirty-Six Out of Sixteen Thousand Refugees Recognized

But, for all that, there were even more refugees in Greece. Since the European border control agency Frontex and national border guard authorities have begun to control the sea border with Turkey, the Middle East, and North Africa (not least through an agreement by ex-Premier Silvio Berlusconi with his ex-friend Muammar Gaddafi of Libya), the smugglers have sought out a new eye-of-the-needle: the relatively impassable border between Turkey and Greece, along the Evros River. What I saw there during my visit in October 2010 reminded me greatly of earlier experiences on the Austrian-Slovakian border along the River March. Except that there it was not 20 or 30 people who crossed the river at night, but 200 or 300! Statistics showed that in 2008 about 50 percent of all arrests of irregular immigrants in the EU took place in Greece. The UN High Commissioner for Refugees (UNHCR) and the Greek Interior Minister Christos Papoutsis (who, tellingly, was called the "Minister for the Protection of Citizens") joined in assuring me that the statistic had risen to 75 percent, and even in the first nine months of 2010 to 90 percent! In other words, the very nation that was combating the threat of bankruptcy was obligated, thanks to the Dublin Regulation, to process the lion's share of the asylum applicants, who came to Europe from Chechnya, Iran, Iraq, Syria, Afghanistan, Pakistan, and other Asian countries, plus some from African countries such as Somalia. For many years there has been overwhelming criticism from UNHCR and experts of Greece's asylum processing system, on account of its low standards, lack of interpreters, and slight chances of anyone being accepted for asylum. Greece had by far the lowest acceptance rate of any European nation. It was not far from 0 percent! In 2009, a total of thirty-six refugees had received asylum out of sixteen thousand applicants.

Flight over the Evros

Long before the crisis of the European asylum policy of 2015 and 2016 was leading to re-nationalization and a genuine crisis of the EU in general, we witnessed already during our Greek mission in October 2010 that the common European Asylum and Migration Policy had failed. What we saw in the police and border control posts of Soufli, Orestiada, and Feres, and in the special detention centers for migrants in Venna and Fylakio in the Evros border region, and in the cells at Venizelos Airport in Athens, as well as in most police stations in Athens, was beyond description. According to Frontex, the number of people who had crossed the Evros River by irregular means rose 369 percent between January and September of 2010. Austria made available to Frontex not only experienced officials, but also buses and infrared cameras and other equipment that was no longer needed along the River March.

In the first two days of our mission alone, 1,400 people were detained and interned. Police officials in Feres personally took us to a spot on the Evros River where 150 people had crossed during the previous night. Wet clothing belonging to people who had been placed in overfilled boats on the other side of the river was strewn about. Many had to swim, although it was quite cool at night at this time of the year. The smugglers told the people to hide in the underbrush during the night, and to start out at dawn and go a couple of kilometers until they found a UN refugee camp, where they would be gladly taken in, fed, and taken care of as refugees with full rights equal to European citizens. On the way back we found six Afghan youths wandering the road in the direction of Feres. They had no fear of the police, and merrily climbed into the police car that would bring them to the UN.

Of course, contrary to what they had been told by smugglers, the refugees found themselves in totally overcrowded, dirty, utterly substandard and inhumane conditions of detention, in police cells or detention centers.

The Detention Cells

The border control post in Feres had two large cells, each furnished with fourteen mattresses for a maximum of twenty-eight detainees. On the day of our visit, 14 October 2010, we found 123 detainees atrociously crammed together. Although the young chief of police at this post, Spyridou Daskaris, tried to care for the detainees as well as possible, his people truly faced an impossible task. There were too few blankets, and the roof of one cell leaked so that it rained inside. The showers and toilets no longer worked, and the cleaning staff from a private firm were not willing to go inside the cells or to clean the toilets, out of fear of the masses of people inside. Instead of performing that duty they cleaned the offices of the officials, all piled to the ceiling with documents. Meanwhile, these officials complained that it was their duty to detain illegal immigrants, not to look after whole families of refugees for months at a time.

We observed quite the same picture in all the establishments that we visited over the next few days; however, the attitudes of the policemen varied tremendously. Not all of them were as agreeable and professional as Spyridou Daskaris. The migrant detention center in Venna with its four large cells for more than two-hundred detainees was a jerry-rigged barn. Venna brought back unfortunate memories of the Serbian concentration camps in northwest Bosnia during the ethnic cleansing. The freezing, teeth-gnashing, and desperate men behind the bars were so beside themselves with anger that it required long discussions and explanations on our part before they would open up to us so that we could enter the cells for private interviews. The four cells had nothing more to offer than bare cement floors and cement flatbeds, often without mattresses and adequate blankets. In front there was nothing but bars, so that it would get quite cold at night. Moreover, all night a glaring spotlight would be aimed at the men, disturbing their sleep. The men were separated by nationality insofar as that was possible. Palestinians, Syrians, and Iraqis were in Cell 1, Chechens and Georgians in Cell 4, and in between were Iranians, Algerians, and many others.

After Being Set Free

As far as we were able to ascertain, these people were genuine refugees, but few of them had faith in applying for asylum. They had heard that applying for asylum would provide them with protection against deportation to Turkey (and subsequent further deportation back to their homelands); however, during that asylum process of many months' duration they would have to remain in detention. On the other hand, if they did not submit an application for asylum they faced the risk of being deported, but stood a greater chance of being set free for a couple of weeks, during which time they might be able to make their way to Western Europe. It was not easy for us to give them sensible advice because the things that they had heard were basically true. The asylum process had become a total fiasco, and the chances of a good outcome for the severely traumatized refugees via that process were as good as nil.

In fact, the authorities did not really differentiate between refugees and immigrants. All detained people were kept in detention until the detention centers were so overfilled that they had to be set free. The selection of those detainees who were to be set free took place either totally arbitrarily or on the basis of the detainees' nationality. People who could not be sent back to their country of origin, such as Afghans, Pakistanis, or Palestinians, were often set free within just a few days with a document that granted them legal residence in Greece for one month. If they had enough money they could make their way to Western Europe, until such time as they were picked up there and sent back to Greece on the basis of the Dublin Regulation. Those who did not have enough money would try their luck with ducking under the radar in Athens. There was essentially no state support at all for anybody in need of assistance. So the only options for these people, who for the most part slept on the streets of Athens, were begging, finding illegal employment, or drifting into crime. It goes without saying that this situation provided rightist-populist parties with ammunition for xenophobic hate campaigns. Violent confrontations between bands of racist thugs and the "illegals" became daily occurrences in neighborhoods of Athens such as Agiou Panteleimonos.

Refugees in Wealthy Europe

I was particularly shaken by the conditions in the migrant detention center of Fylakio near Orestiada. It had only been built a few years earlier, expressly as an "initial intake" center for people who had crossed the Turkish-Greek border by irregular means. However, in the meantime even this modern center had completely gone to wrack and ruin. On the day of our visit, 12 October 2010, 486 people were being kept there, and they were not only men but also entire families with many women and children.

The night before, about 200 people had been picked up in this area. Most of them were still standing in a long line, waiting patiently to be registered and fingerprinted for the Eurodac data bank. We spoke with families from Iran, Afghanistan, and Somalia. They were still completely convinced that they were in a refugee camp administered by the UNHCR rather than in police custody. They believed that after their registration by the police they would be taken in by UN authorities, recognized as refugees, and then provided for accordingly. The fact that we were wearing UN insignia reinforced their hope, hope which we unfortunately had to dash.

When registration was over and they were brought to their overfilled "initial intake" cells, many of them simply broke down and cried. The cell block was equipped with bunk beds, but there was far too little room for the many people. Newcomers had to sleep on the floor, and there were not enough mattresses and blankets. The cleaning staff had refused to clean the toilets and showers for weeks. The toilets were completely clogged and overflowing. A channel of water, urine, and fecal matter ran under the lavatory door into the dormitory where people slept on the floor. The stench was almost unbearable. I dared to make my way on tiptoe into the corridor where the toilets were. There the water full of urine and feces stood five centimeters high and sloshed against me. I quickly closed the door.

And that's the way refugees are welcomed to wealthy Europe in the twenty-first century. That was the thought that ran through my head. Women stood with their sick children in their arms, exhausted from months of flight, and silently wept. They had not imagined Europe to be like this. But there was no going back, since in Afghanistan or Somalia they had given up everything and had given their meager life savings to smugglers. I could offer them little consolation, and felt ashamed to be a European.

Inhumane Conditions

In Athens the situation was not the least bit better. The police stations that we visited had, of necessity, been turned into detention centers for foreigners. Since the cells were overfilled, many people were kept in the offices of the criminal police without registration, a fact that authorities attempted to keep from us. The conditions in police stations like Acropolis and Agiou Panteleimonos beggared description, and could perhaps only be described as inhuman. The same held true for the police stations at Venizelos International Airport, where there were held, among others, those refugees who had been sent back to Greece from Austria and other EU states on the basis of the Dublin Regulation, without checking their asylum status. While the conditions of families, women, and children were acceptable at the time of our visit, the sector in which single men were held was hopelessly overcrowded. It consisted of a long corridor and nine cells, which were intended for two detainees each, and thus a total of eighteen detainees. On the day of our visit, 16 October 2010, we found eighty-eight detainees there. According to the UNHCR, shortly before that there were up to 130 men stuffed into these little cells. And for all of these men there were a total of two toilets and showers on the other side of the corridor. Since the showers were not separated from the toilets, the showers could hardly be used due to time constraints.

Moreover, they were given neither soap nor towels. Most of the men that we talked to had not yet had even one opportunity to shower, and they had been there for as long as a month. Access to the toilets was strictly controlled. In the morning and in the evening each cell in its turn was opened, to give the detainees access to the toilets. Whoever in the meantime needed to urinate, or take care of his other bodily need, made use of plastic bottles and plastic bags, which were then tossed out of the window at the end of the cells, into an outdoor walkway.

I couldn't help but be reminded of the cells in Equatorial Guinea and Jamaica. The officials here seemed to be concerned, but like those in Feres they were simply overwhelmed by the great numbers of detainees. Considering the overcrowding of the detainee cells, it was truly hard to understand why, among the detainees, we found more than a few who were interned here after being held up by the authorities because they lacked a valid entry stamp in their passport, even though they had a perfectly good ticket back to their home countries such as Egypt or Georgia. Now they had no idea where they would get the money to replace the ticket that was expiring while they were obliged to sit out an administrative sentence under these horrible conditions. We could understand all too well why these people were beside themselves with rage.

The Need for a New Refugee Policy

Of course, the Greek authorities and politicians are primarily responsible for these inhumane conditions. After all, they had instituted no adequate asylum process year after year, and had completely neglected the whole matter of aliens. It would be too easy, as well as misleading, to blame the ongoing financial crisis for this malaise.

On the other hand, the situation in Greece was a drastic means of placing before our eyes the shortcomings of the entire "common" European Asylum and Migration Policy. In my opinion it is an absurd idea (and one that falls on the backs of the refugees) to palm off the main burden for irregular migration (including the carrying out of asylum procedures according to the so-called Florian Principle) on south European and east European nations that lie on the external border of the EU. Therefore, my report to the United

Nations Human Rights Council contains recommendations to the EU and its member states to rethink the whole Asylum and Migration Policy, including the Dublin System, and to immediately discontinue all deportations to Greece that are carried out on the basis of the Dublin Regulation.

Nevertheless, the then Austrian Interior Minister Maria Fekter still insisted on her "right" to send "Dublin refugees" back to Greece. Then the European Court of Human Rights stopped her once and for all. In a startling decision of January 2011 in the *M.S.S. vs Belgium and Greece* case, this court ruled that detention conditions for refugees, as well as their general living conditions in the streets of Athens, were humiliating, and that therefore Belgium had done injury to an Afghan "Dublin refugee" by sending him back to Greece, injury that violated the right not to be treated in an inhuman or degrading manner that was secured by the European Convention on Human Rights.

States were no longer allowed to send people back to Greece under the Dublin Regulation. This was in early 2011 when the "Arab Spring" started, followed by repression against these revolutionary movements, civil wars (e.g., in Libya, Syria, and Yemen), terrorism, and the rise of the Islamic State in this troubled region, all of which caused millions of people to flee their countries, of whom many tried to reach the shores of Europe and thousands died in the Mediterranean Sea. I had hoped that the European Union would not only treat the symptoms of its illness (by spending much money on Greece's border security and enhanced professionalization) but also address its root causes, including the flawed Dublin system, which fostered the egoistic nationalistic interests of its member states and thereby contributed to right-wing populism and xenophobia all over Europe. But very little was done to work toward a genuine "common" European Asylum and Migration Policy based on the principles of solidarity and human rights. When in 2015 hundreds of thousands of refugees, above all from Syria, forced their way via Turkey, Greece, and the "Balkan route" to Austria, Germany, Sweden, and other Western European states, the Dublin system broke down and the European Union found itself in the worst crisis of its "common" Asylum and Migration Policy which threatens the very foundations of the European Union.

CONCLUSIONS

I attempted to select the eighteen countries which I visited on official mission during my six-year mandate in a way that represents the international community of states and that allows for the results of my investigations to yield scientifically valid conclusions about the worldwide practice of torture. Although Asia might appear to be overrepresented, we were able to carry out missions to all of the regions of the world, including the Arab, Central Asian, Pacific, and Caribbean regions. The states we investigated ranged from superpowers like the United States and China to relatively large states such as Indonesia, Kazakhstan, or Nigeria and to relatively small states like Jordan, Togo, Uruguay, Jamaica, and Denmark. We visited dictatorships like Equatorial Guinea, as well as democracies in the EU, communist, and capitalist countries alike, states in armed conflict such as Nepal and Sri Lanka, and countries with breakaway territories like Georgia and Moldova.

The spectrum of outcomes ranged from the complete absence of torture in Denmark and Greenland to the systematic practice of torture in Nepal and Equatorial Guinea, and from absolutely degrading detention conditions in countries like Equatorial Guinea, Nigeria, Uruguay, Jamaica, Mongolia, or China to showcase models like Denmark. Statistically, my eighteen missions and three studies undertaken with other United Nations experts allowed me to closely examine approximately 10 percent of the total number of countries in the world.

Torture in 90 Percent of All States

The results of these fact-finding missions are not exactly encouraging. Although torture is unconditionally prohibited for all states in the world, I nonetheless was able to establish that torture occured in seventeen out of eighteen states, or 90 percent of all states. In a portion of these, isolated cases of torture were detected (e.g., in Austria), but in the majority of states torture is routine, widespread, or even systematic. Equally disturbing are the conditions of detention, which in the majority of our twenty-first-century world can only be described as inhuman and degrading. The fact that conditions of detention in many countries have worsened drastically due to the increase in the number of detainees prompted me to refer to a global detention crisis in my last report to the United Nations.

Torture Victims of the Twenty-First Century

During recent years, I was invited on numerous occasions to speak about my experiences as UN special rapporteur on torture, on the phenomenon of torture in the twenty-first century, its extent, and its root causes. In the course of these events it occurred to me yet again that for most people in the industrialized world, torture is associated with the Middle Ages in Europe or National Socialism or brutal dictatorships on far-off continents where torture is used to suppress political opponents or ethnic or religious minorities. Naturally this form of torture exists and is described time and again in literature or depicted in films. The symbol of Christianity, which we come face to face with on a daily basis in the church, is represented by the form of Jesus Christ, a torture victim on the cross. During my missions and investigation work I did of course meet prisoners who had been severely tortured for political reasons: representatives of democracy movements; Tibetans, Uigurs, and Falun Gong adherents in China; political opponents of the Obiang regime in Equatorial Guinea; or people suspected of armed rebellions or terrorism in Nepal, Sri Lanka, Indonesia, Jordan, Russia, or the United States. But from a statistical point of view, these prominent detainees are a very small minority among the millions of torture survivors in the twenty-first century.

The overwhelming majority of victims are ordinary and for the most part poor people, the homeless, arrested by the police on suspicion of having committed a crime or a minor offense but often arbitrarily or for purely discriminatory reasons, and beaten and tortured until they have confessed to having committed the offense.

The reasons for torture have not actually changed much since the Middle Ages, but torture was a legal means to "establish the truth" at the time, whereas now it is practiced illegally and consequently routinely denied. The methods also have not changed significantly, although the psychological methods have been refined because they are to a certain extent more effective and do not leave behind any physical traces.

Torture Principally Affects the Poor

Then as now, apart from political prisoners, torture holds the dubious honor of being a "privilege of the poor," the disenfranchised, the discriminated and marginalized of our global society. They lack the money, education, or self-confidence to rebel or to request legal assistance. Most suffer quietly, remaining in custody or pretrial detention for many additional months because the courts are not in any hurry to deal with such petty cases. Often they are simply "forgotten" while in detention. Many of these pitiful people we interviewed did not even know if they had been convicted or not. They thought the police had already "convicted" them and just wanted to know how much longer they had to serve. Since they had already signed their confession while in police custody, the formal judgment of the court often amounted to little more than a notarization of the "truth determination" by the police. Moreover, many prisons make no distinction whatsoever between pretrial and convicted detainees. It is because of our investigations that we were able to determine in countless cases that the persons in question had already spent more time in pretrial detention than the maximum custodial sentence they could have received for the crime they were charged with.

Educated or wealthy persons are able to sidestep this sort of fate. They always find a way to buy their freedom by bribing the police, prosecutors, judges, or prison staff, and often legally by posting bail. These persons may also be represented by attorneys. The majority of the thousands of detainees we interviewed were not in fact represented by lawyers, or if they were, then by public attorneys made available by the state as legal counsel. As a rule, these persons usually meet their lawyer for the first time only in the courtroom at their trial.

Little Empathy

When we asked detainees if they had been tortured when they were taken into custody by the police, many just stared at us incredulously. Did we not know that torture was routinely used if one did not confess to whatever the charge was immediately after being detained? But in the end the physical pain endured during the first few days of detention was less horrendous than the awareness that many years of their lives were going down the drain as they remained in degrading conditions in prison, innocent and helpless.

The daily struggle for survival in prison, the fear of violence at the hands of fellow inmates and brutal guards, the fight for the little food available or a cell that was a bit less crowded or less filthy, the fear of insects and communicable diseases, and finally, the despotism and insecurity, all worked to wear many people down and cause depression and mental illnesses. Countless detainees, guilty or not, feel they receive worse treatment than animals, and are forgotten by society.

Indeed, society feels very little empathy for detainees. Many NGOs, the media, and politicians stand up for the rights of children, women, minorities, refugees, the LGBTI community, persons with disabilities, and other disadvantaged groups, but very few support the human rights of detainees. Prison walls do more than just keep prisoners locked up: they also serve to keep society from having to face the fate of detainees. Most people have never actually seen the inside of a prison and do not care to. Many believe that "Someone who is behind bars must have done something wrong" and does not deserve our empathy for this reason alone. This common defense mechanism enables us to simply stop dealing with these people.

What Needs to Be Done?

We know precisely what needs to be done in order to eradicate torture. Years ago Amnesty International put forward a twelve-point program for the prevention of torture that is as relevant and compelling today as it was then. We also know that the implementation of these twelve requirements is anything but vaguely theoretical, unrealistically utopian, or illusory. On the contrary, these are concrete proposals whose transposition into practice has been tried and tested, whose effectiveness has been established, and whose realization is financially achievable—if the necessary political will is there.

Measures to Prevent Torture

Prevention must begin where torture usually occurs, namely during the first few days of police custody. Every single arrest and police custody case must be accurately recorded and documented. Detainees must immediately be able to contact family members, lawyers, and/or medical doctors and must be allowed to speak with them and be visited by them. Every interrogation of a detainee by the police must be documented by video and as a rule must take place in the presence of an attorney.

Police custody should be limited to the shortest possible time and never exceed forty-eight hours. Detainees must then be brought before an independent court, where accusations of torture may be expressed without the presence of police forces and without fear of reprisals. If an accusation of torture is made or there is reason to suspect it, or there are indications that torture has taken place, an investigation by independent forensic medical experts must immediately follow. Under no circumstances should detainees be returned to the police by the court. Only if there are reasonable grounds to suspect that a person has committed an offense and there are special additional grounds, such as the danger of re-offending, collusion, or flight, may the court impose pretrial detention. However, the pretrial detention must be served in a prison that is subordinated to judicial authorities (and not under the police or Ministry of the Interior).

In pretrial detention, it should at all times be possible to lodge a complaint regarding torture or abuse and to have such a complaint investigated by a medical forensic expert. Pretrial detention should not be the rule, but rather the exception, as there are other methods to ensure that a suspect does not escape justice. Among these are the confiscation of a suspect's passport, posting bail, or using electronic cuffs. If pretrial detention is ordered on an exceptional basis, it should not exceed six months.

Unannounced Visits

If all of these rules, which are already for the most part included in international human rights treaties, were heeded, the risk of torture could be reduced to a minimum at an acceptable cost. A lack of political will explains why more progress has not been achieved. In 2002, the adoption of the OPCAT (Optional Protocol to the UN Convention Against Torture), after more than two decades of fierce debates in the United Nations Human Rights Commission, opened a new opportunity to effectively prevent torture and improve conditions of detention. Admittedly the cost implications are much higher: the setting up of National Preventive Mechanisms, which are commissions made up of experts in a number of different disciplines. These experts would have the right, unannounced and at any time, to inspect all places of detention (including police lockups), to hold confidential interviews with all detainees, and to have detainees examined by medical forensic experts. Not only is such a system expensive, but it would represent a paradigm shift for many states to the extent that dark police cells and torture chambers would suddenly be subjected to public scrutiny and transparency.

The extreme persistence of torture is explained by the fact that it always takes place in the dark, in seclusion, in secret. In most states the intelligence services, military, and police are simply unaccustomed to having independent human rights observers looking over their shoulders as they work. This would seriously interfere with their effectiveness in combating crime, one hears repeatedly. In reality this attitude is nothing more than the adherence to a police culture that is beyond the reach of the rule of law and human rights. Effective National Preventive Mechanisms have the potential to convert the paradigm of obscurity into one of transparency. Whether they will succeed depends on the political will of governments and their security forces.

Combating the Impunity of Torture

The fight against impunity for torturers is just as important as the prevention of torture via relevant rule-of-law guarantees and regular visits to places of detention by independent inspectors. Torture is currently sanctioned, if at all, as a trivial or minor offense at most punishable by a mild disciplinary measure and not, as set forth in the United Nations Convention against Torture, by a long prison term for both torturers and their principals.

The Austrian case of Bakary Jassey represents a typical example of this type of attitude within the police, the judiciary, and in politics. A very basic change needs to be made to this attitude, involving nothing more than finally implementing the international obligations of the UN Convention against Torture. The first step is the establishment of a stand-alone criminal offense for the crime of torture with a commensurate penalty, as is the case for murder, robbery, and other comparable violent crimes. The second step requires the courts to acknowledge that torture is not merely a forgivable misdemeanor but is in fact one of the most brutal, violent crimes and often leads to traumatization with long-term effects for the victims. In cases where torture is proven, the courts should apply the appropriate penalty range to the fullest and not show excessive leniency toward a states' security forces.

The main reason for the widespread impunity for torturers is the difficulty of finding and documenting evidence of torture and abuse by security forces which are sufficient for a criminal conviction. As is true in most countries, there are numerous accusations of abuse against the police in Austria but practically no criminal convictions. Generally, such cases do not even get as far as a trial because the Public Prosecutor's Office discontinues almost all legal proceedings for lack of evidence and does not even bring charges against the police officer in question. Why? Because investigations of the police are carried out by the police, and their esprit de corps, not only in Austria, is much stronger than their readiness to hand over the "black sheep" from their own ranks to judicial authorities. A police officer who has struck or tortured a detainee during an interrogation will always find fellow officers who will testify that the victim fell down the stairs or suffers from self-inflicted injuries. Torture and abuse will continue to go unpunished and without consequences until this attitude experiences a radical change.

Hence my mantra-like demands made to so many governments to set up dedicated complaint, investigation, and prosecution authorities, independent of the police, to deal with torture, ill-treatment, arbitrary executions, and other violent crimes perpetrated by state security forces. It is essential that such authorities possess the same investigative power and expertise as the criminal police, but with full operational autonomy. Counterarguments I have frequently heard stress that it is inconceivable to set up a dedicated criminal police unit to investigate members of security forces that would also have the authority to detain and/or search police officers, monitor their mobile telephones, and so on.

At the same time in many countries there are dedicated complaint, investigation, and prosecution authorities with the necessary expertise to be able to deal with corruption by state officials. It would appear that corruption is considered to be a more serious issue than torture. This may well be because any of us can suffer at the hands of corrupt officials, whereas victims of torture are usually only "criminals" whose credibility is considered by most to be questionable.

"Only" Detainees

The fundamental question we must now consider is: Why is it so difficult to eradicate torture and improve conditions of detention? One of the most important explanations is the lack of empathy toward those who for whatever reason are behind bars. The presumption of innocence is a fundamental principle of criminal justice. A suspect is innocent until convicted by a court. But what happens in practice is the exact opposite. A person who is detained by the police because he or she is suspected of having committed a criminal act is considered guilty by most people, by politicians, and the media. And the guilty do not deserve sympathy.

As long as our security benefits from it, criminals can be detained by the police a little longer than is allowed, they can be handled a little more firmly than necessary and, if need be, tortured just a little. In the United States the Bush administration and its allies in the media and among scientists used the thought experiment about the "dirty bomb" and the incantation about the primacy of national security interests to convince large segments of the population that in the fight against terrorism, torture was the lesser evil. In Europe too, many people fell for this trick and as a result, torture has lost much of its "terror" aspect and has become somewhat accepted. Fear and hatred have always made good politics. In the end, it does not make much of a difference anymore if our craving for security is threatened by terrorists, organized crime, or "ordinary criminals."

The Danish Model

Denmark provides the best example of how torture can be eradicated if the authorities treat detainees with empathy and consider them as clients rather than inmates. In my work as UN special rapporteur on torture, the only country where there was no torture and at the same time by far the best detention conditions was Denmark, including Greenland. Before visiting Denmark, I lived in Sweden and had an opportunity to visit prisons there, which I found were comparable to those in Denmark. I believe that the Nordic countries have generally succeeded in practically eliminating torture.

What are the Nordic countries doing that is different from most other countries including Europe? Is it exclusively linked to the well-known elevated degree of development, democracy, and rule of law? Clearly, these factors play a decisive role, but I believe that the justice and criminal law philosophy espoused by the general public is just as important. For instance, the United States is a comparatively highly developed rule-of-law democracy, but with a marked tendency in the population to turn justice and politics into retributive justice in the Old Testament sense of "an eye for an eye, a tooth for a tooth." This is why Americans continue to defend the death penalty tooth and nail, contrary to all rational arguments, and also why the United States is the country with the highest rate of detainees worldwide (eight hundred out of one hundred thousand inhabitants, whereas the West European average is approximately one hundred per one hundred thousand) and also why conditions of detention in the United States are far more inhuman than in Europe. The logic is that someone who has committed a crime must face commensurate atonement and suffering. Far from achieving the intended deterrent effect, this attitude contributes to a high level of violence and crime in the population and also fosters a public endorsement of torture. The United States is the best example of this cause and effect relationship.

The "principle of normalization" as practiced in Danish prisons is the antithesis to the American retributive criminal justice system. The idea is that the detainee should thrive as opposed to feeling punished in every respect. Even if detainees have committed a crime, they are not seen as dangerous criminals first and foremost who represent a security risk and must be isolated to the maximum extent possible from society or even eliminated. Rather, they continue to enjoy the status of human beings with rights and duties like all others. They are people who may have committed a wrongful act but one that they can make up for; they are people who, after serving their custodial sentence, need help to reintegrate into society without committing another crime. Today, international law recognizes the principle according to which a custodial sentence should not serve the purposes of retribution but should aim to rehabilitate detainees, leading to a reduction in recidivism and crime. Nonetheless, many societies and especially those in which religion plays a significant role find it very difficult to move from retributive criminal justice to a modern human rights–based criminal justice system. I firmly believe that this is a crucial prerequisite for more empathy toward detainees and a decreased risk of torture.

The Poverty Factor

Clearly, other factors such as poverty, underdevelopment, corruption, lack of rule of law, and a professional judiciary all play an important role in the global prison crisis and the widespread practice of torture. When almost two-thirds of the population have no genuine access to the rule of law and to an at least partially functional judiciary, as has been established by the International Commission on the Legal Empowerment of the Poor, the result is that torture and inhuman detention conditions remain a "privilege of the poor." In many poor countries only radical strategies aimed at fighting global poverty, reforming the justice system, and ensuring equal access through "legal empowerment" of the poor and eradicating corruption can bring about a durable improvement in conditions of detention and a successful fight against torture. Hence my appeal to international development agencies to attach the highest priority to the "legal empowerment" of the poor, the formation of professional and corruption-free structures in the judiciary, and increased efforts to combat torture and improve prison conditions.

At the same time, however, the poverty of a country must never be abused as a justification for torture and brutal conditions in places of detention. A good many of the poorest states have shown that the acceptance of a modern criminal justice philosophy has done much more to improve prison conditions and lower the risk of torture than building expensive, modern, high-security prisons with resources from poorly conceived development cooperation efforts.

Rights versus Revenge

Although we know what needs to happen in order to eradicate torture worldwide, and although many of the measures needed do not require vast amounts of funding and are already laid down in international law, it would be illusory to believe that torture can be eliminated in the foreseeable future. The reason is that the criminal justice philosophy based on revenge and retribution is much too deeply rooted in the world's religions and thereby also in the sense of righteousness of people and societies in the North and in the South, in poor and in rich countries, to allow for a rapid change of attitude.

In spite of everything, I remain an optimist. I can explain my optimism by pointing to the success of the global human rights movement as regards the abolition of the death penalty, which is virtually a symbol of retributive justice. When the United Nations proclaimed the Universal Declaration of Human Rights in 1948, capital punishment was on the books in just about every country in the world and was being imposed and executed. Today, thanks to the tireless awareness-raising work of Amnesty International, the European Union, and other organizations, it has been de jure or at least de facto abolished in two-thirds of the countries in the world. This cruel punishment is frowned upon today in Europe and Latin America. In addition, many countries in Africa and some in Asia have followed this example and each year, two or three countries are added to the list of those that have abolished the death penalty. This reversal of opinion has prompted the United Nations General Assembly to call on all states to at least declare a moratorium on the death penalty, in spite of fierce opposition from powerful governments like the United States, China, and a number of Islamic states. A similar development is evident in the area of corporal punishment, which today is prohibited in most countries of the world, not only as a judicial and disciplinary sanction, but also in schools and within families. This is an indication that human rights, embedded in international law and generally prohibiting all cruel, inhuman, and degrading treatment and punishment, are gradually gaining the upper hand over retributive criminal justice. Let's hope that the trend toward abolition of corporal and capital punishment will also lead to the gradual elimination of torture, one of the most brutal human rights violations of our time.

INDEX

ACKNOWLEDGMENTS

After six years as UN special rapporteur on torture between 2004 and 2010, I summarized my impressions and experience from eighteen official fact-finding missions and a few joint investigations with other UN experts in a book written in German, my mother tongue, entitled *Folter—Die Alltäglichkeit des Unfassbaren* (Verlag Kremayr & Scheriau KG, Vienna). I was repeatedly urged by friends and colleagues to also publish an English translation. After Roger Kaminker, a senior and highly experienced UN interpreter who had accompanied me on a number of these fact-finding missions, offered to translate the book, I finally agreed. Since we had become close friends during these missions, he was able to provide me with an excellent translation which captured the personal spirit in which this book was written. I am very grateful to Roger for his insistence and kind assistance. As far as this seemed appropriate, I updated the book. In particular, I added my follow-up experience based upon an EU-funded project carried out together with my team at the Ludwig Boltzmann Institute of Human Rights in Vienna, aimed at assisting a number of selected governments willing to implement my recommendations after the respective fact-finding missions. I also wish to warmly thank Bert Lockwood for his offer to publish this book with the University of Pennsylvania Press.

All of the facts and findings on which this book is based have already been published in my official reports to the United Nations. I felt it was important to add more personal thoughts and feelings experienced during these missions which I could not express in my official reports to the United Nations. I am very grateful to the governments of these eighteen countries in all world regions for their kind invitation to carry out official fact-finding missions and their willingness to allow me to conduct unannounced visits of many places of detention and confidential interviews with detainees, torture survivors and witnesses. Without their consent, I would not have been able to gather such a deep insight into the extent of the practice of torture and the conditions of detention in our current world order. In seventeen of the eighteen states visited (with the only exception of Denmark and Greenland) I found evidence of torture, and I was shocked by the inhuman and degrading conditions of detention in all regions of the world.

Fact-finding missions are always a collective exercise, and their success depends on the quality of the teams which prepared these missions, accompanied me during these visits, and assisted me in preparing my UN reports. I was very lucky to have been able to rely always on excellent collaborators from the Office of the UN High Commissioner for Human Rights (OHCHR) in Geneva and on a small team of experts at the Vienna-based Ludwig Boltzmann Institute of Human Rights (BIM), funded by voluntary contributions of the governments of Austria, Switzerland, Germany, and Liechtenstein. First of all, I wish to express my deep gratitude to the following human rights officers of the OHCHR: Safir Syed, Birgit Kainz-Labbé, Claudia de la Fuente, Stephanie Kleine-Ahlbrandt, Anna Crawford, and Sonia Cronin. In Uruguay, Silvia da Rin Pagnetto and Juan-Miguel Petit from the UN country team joined our visits to places of detention, as did Mathilde Bogner and Christina Saunders in Papua New Guinea. Both in the preparation, conduct and follow-up to the missions, the UN staff worked in close cooperation with the following members of the BIM-team to whom I am equally grateful: Julia Kozma, Elizabeth McArthur, Naoimh Hughes, Roland Schmidt, Isabelle Tschan, Johanna Lober, Tiphanie Crittin, and Moritz Birk. I was also very fortunate to have been accompanied by some of the leading forensic experts in the world: Duarte Nuno Vieira, Derrick Pounder, Hans-Petter Hougen, Jonathan Beynon, and Máximo Duque. Without them, much of the evidence which we had gathered through interviews with detainees and witnesses could not have been corroborated. On most missions we were also accompanied by excellent interpreters, such as Roger Kaminker. Finally, I wish to thank all the other members of our teams, including the UN resident coordinators, our UN security officers, our drivers, and other local UN staff who contributed to the safe and well-organized conduct of our missions. Finally, I wish to thank my colleagues at the University of Vienna, Georges Younes, Marijana Grandits, Hugo Bittencourt, and Gala Gloria Rak, for their thoughtful comments and assistance in finalizing the English version of this book. Notwithstanding all the valuable teamwork and assistance which I have received in conducting my mandate as UN special rapporteur on torture and in writing this book, I wish to stress that all the findings of my missions and all thoughts expressed in this book are my sole responsibility.

I dedicate this book to the many torture survivors who were kind and brave enough to share their horrific experiences with me. Whatever they might have done, they truly deserve a world without torture and with humane conditions of detention. It is my deep conviction that such a world would be possible if governments were willing to fully implement their respective obligations under international human rights law.

Lightning Source UK Ltd.
Milton Keynes UK
UKHW041701031220
374203UK00025B/86/J